NEW FOREST

& the SOUTH OF ENGLAND

Short Break Guide

The South of England, like so many other regions of Britain, is unique. For the purposes of this guide, the South is defined as the whole of Hampshire, Dorset and Wiltshire, but parts of Somerset are also included. The New Forest, in Hampshire, offers visitors a pleasant and convenient centre from which to tour this beautiful, richly varied area of England.

NAVAL TRADITIONS

The area has a long tradition of providing a home to Britain's navy. The sheltered harbours of Southampton and, more particularly, nearby Portsmouth, provided safe havens for the royal fleet, especially from Tudor times onwards. The forest also provided the timber needed to build warships, and places such as Buckler's Hard became famous as ship-building centres.

MYSTERIOUS PAST

The South of England, particularly Wiltshire and Dorset, has a greater concentration of prehistoric sites than any other comparable area in the country. They range from simple burial mounds and massive Iron Age hillforts (such as Maiden Castle) to stone chamber tombs (such as the Kennet Long Barrow) and massive stone circles, like Avebury and Stonehenge (see pages 21 and 26 respectively). Many of these monuments, which date from the Stone Age and Bronze Age through to the Iron Age, are shrouded in mystery, largely because of our lack of understanding about the societies that built them. What these sites do tell us, however, is that Britain was peopled by a very sophisticated civilization long before the Roman occupation.

LANDSCAPES

The landscapes of Southern England are as rich as they are varied. They range from the downlands of north Hampshire and the open grassland plains of Wiltshire, to the deeply folded and hilly landscape of Dorset. The New Forest, in Hampshire, is one of the largest tracts of forest and heathland in England and is still protected by ancient forest laws. The coastal regions, particularly the fossil-rich cliffs of Dorset, are magnificent and still largely unspoilt.

LITERARY CONNECTIONS

The South of England, particularly Dorset, is often referred to as 'Thomas Hardy country'. The area has many associations with this famous Victorian novelist, whose stories centre on the ordinary country folk of the past. Much of the landscape described in Hardy's novels can still be seen today. He was born in 1840 at Higher Bockhampton and spent most of his life in Dorset (his cottage is shown left). In his novels, Dorchester became 'Casterbridge', Weymouth 'Budmouth Regis', Bournemouth 'Sandborne' and Salisbury 'Melchester'.

The adjacent county of Hampshire has close associations with another literary giant, Jane Austen, noted for her domestic novels of manners. Born in Steventon in 1775, Austen lived in Southampton for several years before finally settling at Chawton. She died in Winchester in 1817 and is buried in the cathedral.

CLIMATE

Southern England benefits from a below-average record of rainfall, compared to most other regions of the country. This is coupled with a higher-than-average record of sunshine. Sheltered from the worst of the storms that frequently ravage the Southwest, the area has become one of Britain's favourite holiday destinations. Much of the underlying rock is chalk, which drains rapidly even after heavy rainfall, allowing grass and cereal crops to flourish on the wide, open expanses to the north of the region.

THE NEW FOREST

Of the many landscape features associated with this area, probably the most famous is the New Forest. This vast area of woodland and heath covers about 90,000 acres (36,400 hectares) in all (see pages 22–23). Large parts of it are maintained by the Forestry Commission, and about two-thirds of the area is open to the public. The land was designated a royal forest by William I (William the Conqueror) who appropriated it as an exclusive hunting ground in 1079. It has always been protected by special laws, including the right of commoners to graze their ponies and livestock in certain areas.

The beaches of Southern England are among the best in the country. Blessed with fine sands, spectacular coastal scenery, clean safe waters and the highest sunshine records in England, they have become extremely popular with holidaymakers. Whether you are in search of quiet, deserted coves or a bustling, commercial resort, there is plenty of choice.

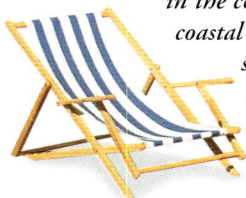

1 LYME REGIS, DORSET

Lyme Regis has several beaches, all a mixture of sand and shingle, backed by dramatic cliff scenery. Lyme is not a traditional seaside resort, but it is one of the most stylish towns on the South coast. Centred around its ancient harbour, it still resembles a large fishing village, reminiscent of those more commonly found in Cornwall.

The town gained international acclaim as the setting for the film *The French Lieutenant's Woman,* which used the famous 14th-century breakwater, known as the Cobb, as its central setting. Bathing is generally safe, except near the harbour area. Facilities in the town are excellent, yet the town lacks the usual brashness of seaside resorts.

P WC ⦿ ♿   🚃 - Axminster

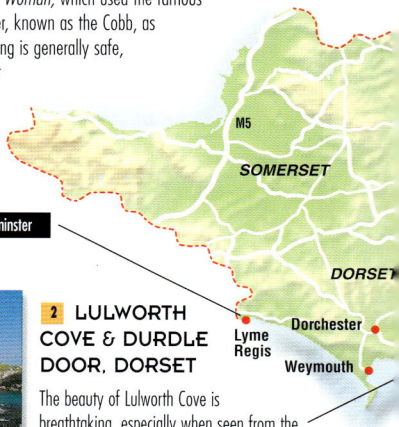

M5

SOMERSET

DORSET

2 LULWORTH COVE & DURDLE DOOR, DORSET

Lyme Regis

Dorchester

Weymouth

The beauty of Lulworth Cove is breathtaking, especially when seen from the cliffs above. The bay is protected by two arms of rock that form a natural amphitheatre, and seems almost tropical with its fine sands and clear, blue water. The cove, along with the nearby Durdle Door (a natural arch cut into the rocks by the action of the tides) has a complex geological structure and there are excellent cliff-top walks along the Dorset Coastal Path. Facilities at the cove have been carefully limited to preserve its charm, but the village of West Lulworth is only a short drive away.

P WC ⦿ ♿ (imited access)   🚃 - Wool

3 STUDLAND, DORSET

Studland village and its associated bay are quiet havens in what can be a busy coastal playground in the summer months. The village, with its celebrated unrestored Norman church, remains quite unspoilt. There are many quiet lanes and footpaths leading to the sandy beach owned by the National Trust. The shallow waters of the bay prevent larger craft from landing, but provide safe bathing in clean waters.

P WC ⦿ ♿   🚃 - Wareham

4 SWANAGE, DORSET

Situated a few miles south of Poole Harbour, the beaches lining Swanage Bay are a haven for bathers. The waters are generally safe, except at Ballard Point to the north of the bay, and Peveril Ledge to the south, where the cliffs can be treacherous. Boats can be hired at Swanage Pier for deep-sea fishing trips, and nearby there are diving and windsurfing schools and fine shops. The beaches at Swanage are sandy and the cliffs offer many sheltered inlets, where the waters are among the warmest in the country.

P WC ⑩ & 🚂 - Wareham

5 HAYLING ISLAND, HAMPSHIRE

Situated at the eastern extremity of Hampshire, Hayling Island lies just west of Chichester Harbour. Permanently linked to the mainland by a bridge, the island has a vast seaside resort and 4 miles (6 km) of sandy beach on its southern shore. Despite having all the trappings of the modern resort, there are still large areas of unspoilt marshland and dunes at the two extremities. Water sports are popular at Hayling, including water-skiing, windsurfing and sailing as well as safe bathing.

P WC ⑩ & 🚂 - Havant

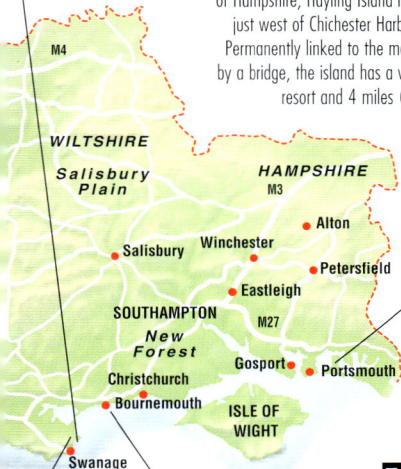

6 BOURNEMOUTH, DORSET

Sometimes considered the queen of British holiday resorts, Bournemouth offers an excellent range of facilities and entertainment to suit all tastes. While many resorts have become over-commercialized, Bournemouth has arguably retained a great deal of its charm and elegance. Until the arrival of the railway in 1870, this resort was little more than a quiet, residential seaside town, but since then it has grown significantly. It boasts 7 miles (11 km) of sandy beaches, with safe bathing. Regularly patrolled by lifeguards, the beaches are backed by wide promenades and beautiful, tree-clad cliffs, several theatres, parks and every conceivable holiday entertainment.

P WC ⑩ & 🚂 - Bournemouth

THE SAXON SHORE

Towards the end of the Roman occupation of this country, Britain began to suffer attacks by Saxon pirates from northern Europe. To protect the shores of eastern and southern England, a series of at least nine forts were built along the coast, from Brancaster in Norfolk to Portchester in Hampshire. They were instigated by Carausius, self-styled Emperor of Britain, between AD 287–293 and came to be known as Forts of the Saxon Shore.

7 MILFORD-ON-SEA, HAMPSHIRE

Milford-on-Sea is a predominantly modern residential town a few miles east of Bournemouth. The beach is a mixture of shingle, with sand at low tide, and provides a quiet alternative to the hustle and bustle of its larger and more commercial neighbours. The town offers good facilities in the form of toilets, cafés and beach shops, but little else. The neighbouring small resorts of Barton-on-Sea and Highcliffe offer similar facilities, with safe bathing in some of Europe's cleanest waters. *(Note that some car parks are located on the cliff tops and require a short walk to the beach.)*

P WC ¶O¹ & 🚌 - New Milton

8 WEYMOUTH, DORSET

Weymouth became fashionable as a seaside resort in 1789, when George III visited the town and became the first monarch to use a bathing machine. Although it has grown considerably and is now one of the finest resorts on the south coast, Weymouth still retains much of its Georgian elegance. Regular ferry services run between the harbour, the French coast and the Channel Islands. Weymouth offers excellent visitor facilities with a long, sheltered, sandy beach. Bathing and water sports facilities are good. Nearby are the ruins of Sandsfoot Castle, built by Henry VIII as part of his scheme of coastal protection from overseas invaders.

P WC ¶O¹ & 🚌 - Weymouth

M5

SOMERSET

DORSET

Lyme Regis

Dorcheste

Weymouth

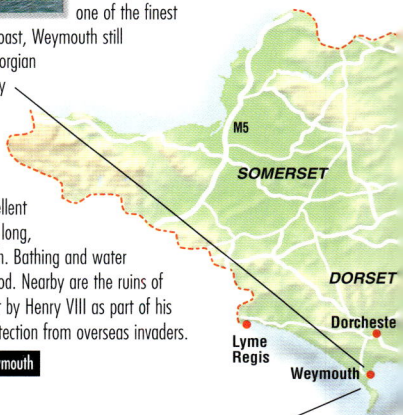

9 CHESIL BEACH & PORTLAND BILL, DORSET

Dorset is rich in geological oddities, a fine example being Chesil Beach. Some 10 miles (16 km) long and over 40 ft (13 metres) high in places, this remarkable beach forms a huge shingle bank running parallel to the coast, with a sheltered lagoon (known as the Fleet) behind. It terminates at the Isle of Portland, another interesting geological feature formed from a huge table of limestone jutting out into the sea, much favoured as a quality building stone. The waters at Portland can be quite ferocious and are not suitable for bathing, although Chesil Beach offers good sunbathing. The pebbles here apparently absorb a large amount of the sun's heat and create a mild sub-climate.

P WC ¶O¹ & 🚌 - Weymouth

10 CALSHOT, HAMPSHIRE

Calshot lies at the southwestern-most tip of Southampton Water. To the west lies Buckler's Hard and the New Forest, and to the south, the Solent. Although the beach here is pebble rather than sand, it provides perfect water for safe bathing and water sports. Nearby are the peaceful acres of Calshot Country Park, an ideal spot for a picnic. Calshot became famous in the early years of this century as a centre for maritime air training. The RAF air base closed in 1961, and the buildings were taken over by Hampshire County Council.

P WC ⦿ ♿ 🚂 - Brockenhurst

11 SOUTHSEA, HAMPSHIRE

Southsea is now part of Portsmouth, although it still retains its old seaside character. The resort has two piers and all the usual visitor attractions, including boat trips around Portsmouth Harbour. The area is ringed with fortifications, both in the Channel and on land, built from Tudor times onwards to protect the Royal Naval Dockyard. A long shingle beach runs eastwards for several miles, with sand at low tide, offering safe bathing. The beach is regularly patrolled by lifeguards.

P WC ⦿ ♿

🚂 - Portsmouth and Southsea

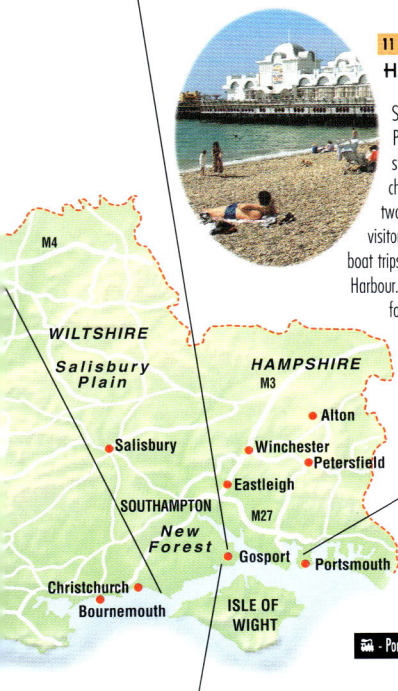

WILTSHIRE
Salisbury Plain
M4
Salisbury
HAMPSHIRE
M3
Alton
Winchester
Petersfield
Eastleigh
SOUTHAMPTON
M27
New Forest
Gosport
Portsmouth
Christchurch
Bournemouth
ISLE OF WIGHT

12 LEPE, HAMPSHIRE

Although not the nicest of Hampshire's beaches (the sand and shingle tend to give way to mud at low tide), the setting is beautiful, with stunning views across the Solent to the Isle of Wight. The beach is excellent for bathing, and the nearby country park has several picnic spots set among the trees. Facilities are somewhat limited, however, and you are advised to take your own refreshments.

P WC ♿ 🚂 - Brockenhurst

The following selection of places to visit has been specially chosen with children in mind, to provide that extra bit of excitement. They range from family days out at leisure complexes to wildlife parks and heritage centres which offer hands-on experience to fuel imaginations.

1 CHOLDERTON RARE BREEDS FARM

Amesbury Road, Cholderton, Salisbury, Wiltshire

Featured several times on radio and television, Cholderton Rare Breeds Farm has been voted 'Best Family Attraction in Wiltshire'. The farm specializes in conserving endangered breeds of farm animals. There are also gardens, a nature trail, picnic areas, adventure playgrounds, tractor and trailer rides and, at weekends and school holidays, the hilarious Park Stakes pig races!
Open daily, end Mar.-end Oct. ☎ 01980 629438

P WC ⊙ ⅄   🚂 - Grateley

2 SEA LIFE CENTRE

Clarence Esplanade, Southsea, Portsmouth, Hampshire

Overlooking the bustling Solent, the Sea Life Centre is an exciting introduction for children to the mysterious world beneath the waves. There are over 30 astonishing hi-tech displays, allowing visitors a unique insight into the lives of creatures such as sharks and conger eels. There is an Explorers' Club, a soft play area, paddling pool, quiz trail, touch pools and baby changing facilities. Open daily all year, except Christmas Day. Reduced opening hours in winter. ☎ 02392 875222 or 02392 734461 *(info line)*

P - nearby WC ⊙ ⅄
🚂 - Portsmouth and Southsea

3 NEW FOREST OWL SANCTUARY

Crow Lane, Crow, Ringwood, Hampshire

The largest collection of owls in Europe is on display at the New Forest Owl Sanctuary. It acts as a breeding and release centre for owls and birds of prey and is not a zoo. There are regular free-flying displays of the birds. The sanctuary offers a great day out for the children, with the emphasis on education and conservation. There are special shaded areas where dog owners can park their cars out of the sun. Open daily Mar.-Nov., then weekends only. ☎ 01425 476487

P WC ⊙ ⅄   🚂 - Bournemouth

4 WATERCRESS LINE

The Station, Alresford, Hampshire

Running through 10 miles (16 km) of beautiful countryside, the Watercress Line steam railway takes visitors on a nostalgic journey back to the 1950s, when steam reigned supreme. Children will love the sights, sounds and smells of the steam engine. There are also special children's events, such as Thomas the Tank Engine and Santa Specials in winter. Originally part of the Southern Region line, which closed in 1973, it has been re-opened in stages, mainly by volunteer organizations. Open weekends Feb.-Oct., and most weekdays end May-early Sept. ☎ 01962 733810 or 01962 734866 *(talking timetable)*

P WC ⚪ ♿ 🚌 - Alton

🚌 - has a footbridge link to platform

5 LONGLEAT

Wiltshire (off the A36 between Salisbury and Bath, A362 between Warminster and Frome)

Longleat includes the premier safari park in the country – the first to be opened (in 1966) outside Africa. Longleat House is the Elizabethan ancestral home of the Marquess of Bath and is well worth a visit; but, for the children, the wild animals are the main attraction. As well as the famous lions, there are tigers, elephants and giraffes. Other attractions include the

world's longest hedge maze, a railway, an adventure castle and safari boats. All attractions open daily, Apr.-Oct. ☎ 01985 844400

P WC ⚪ ♿ 🚌 - Warminster

6 MARWELL ZOOLOGICAL PARK

Colden Common, near Winchester, Hampshire (signposted from M3 & M27 motorways)

Easily accessible from the M3, Marwell Zoological Park is a fun day out for all the family, with a road and rail train, amusements and an adventure playground. You can relax in the delightful 100-acre (40-hectare) park and gardens and marvel at animals from around the world. There are many endangered species, including Siberian tigers, okapi and rhinos. Open daily all year, except Christmas Day. ☎ 01962 777407 or 01426 943163 *(info line)*

P WC ⚪ ♿ 🚌 - Eastleigh or Winchester

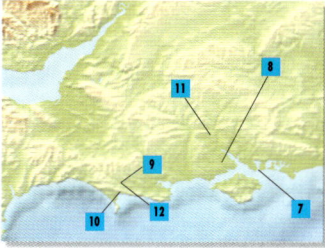

7 THE PYRAMIDS CENTRE, LEISURE COMPLEX

Clarence Esplanade, Southsea, Hampshire

The kids will love Pyramids, Southsea's all-weather leisure complex, featuring tropical pools, wave machine, exciting flume rides, toddlers' pool and much more. Gift shop, inflatables, poolside amusement and video games provide fun for all the family. Open daily throughout the summer (reduced opening during winter). ☎ 02392 799977

🅿 ♿ 🍴 ♿

🚆 - Portsmouth and Southsea

8 NATIONAL MOTOR MUSEUM

John Montagu Building, Beaulieu, Hampshire

Beaulieu is really several attractions in one and represents a classic day out for all the family in the heart of the New Forest. Palace House has been the Montagu family home since 1538, when the 13th-century Beaulieu Abbey was confiscated by Henry VIII and converted into a private house. The monastic ruins now form part of the delightful gardens here. The National Motor Museum, which traces the story of motoring from 1894 to the present day, has more than 250 vehicles on display, including several record breakers. Open daily all year, except Christmas Day. ☎ 01590 612345 or 01590 612123 (info line)

🅿 ♿ 🍴 ♿ 🚆 - Brockenhurst

9 TUTANKHAMUN EXHIBITION

25 High West Street, Dorchester, Dorset

The only example of its kind outside Egypt, the Tutankhamun Exhibition is world renowned for its innovative display techniques, offering a unique experience of rediscovery. Opened

65 years after Howard Carter's discovery of the tomb in 1922, the exhibition enables you to relive the experience using sight, sound and smell, as though actually witnessing the event. In the Hall of Treasures you can see marvellous facsimiles of some of Tutankhamun's greatest golden treasures. Open daily all year, except 24-26 Dec. ☎ 01305 269571

🅿 - nearby ♿

🚆 - Dorchester South and West

10 NOTHE FORT

Barrack Road, Weymouth, Dorset

This fascinating Victorian fort was built in 1860–72 to defend Portland Naval Base from the threat of French invasion. The fort has been fully restored and has over 70 rooms arranged on three levels. It contains many displays, using life-size figures, to show what life was like for the garrison. There are several massive guns on display and a junior assault

course for the children to let off steam. Open daily, mid-May to mid-Sept.

01305 787243

P - nearby ♿ - Weymouth

11 PAULTONS FAMILY LEISURE PARK

Ower, near Romsey, Hampshire (off junction 2 of the M27)

Paultons Family Leisure Park provides an action-packed day out for all the family, with over 40 different attractions included in the ticket price. Choose from the log flume, family roller coaster, bumper boats, Kids Kingdom, Wind in the Willows, special rides for the tots, beautiful gardens for the older members of the family, animals, museums and model dinosaurs! The Romany Experience exhibition includes the country's finest collection of genuine gypsy caravans. Open daily, mid.-Mar.-Oct., then weekends Nov.-Dec. until Christmas. *(Special family tickets available.)*

02380 814442 or 02380 814455 *(info line)* P ♿ - Southampton

12 TEDDY BEAR HOUSE

Antelope Walk, Dorchester, Dorset

This makes an unusual family day out, and is especially good for younger children. Teddy bears of all types and sizes can be seen in realistic displays arranged around the house. Children can also see some human-sized teddy bears and learn the story of the Teddy Bear House. Open daily all year, except 25-26 Dec.

01305 263200 P - nearby
♿ - Dorchester South and West

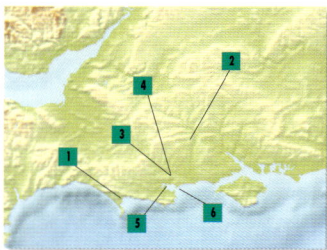

The attractions listed on these pages are ideal for visiting on rainy days. Worth seeing at any time, of course, they offer shelter and a range of indoor facilities that will be welcomed by visitors looking for somewhere to go when the heavens open!

1 WEYMOUTH SEA LIFE PARK

Lodmoor Country Park, Weymouth, Dorset (off the A353, Esplanade)

With stunning displays and state-of-the-art computer technology, Sea Life brings you close to the world of underwater wildlife. Set in spacious grounds, this centre has a good mix of indoor and outdoor attractions. There are themed marine displays covering all aspects of life in the seas, including sharks and octopuses and a range of different habitats. Many educational and hands-on experiences. Open daily all year *(reduced hours in winter)*.

☎ 01305 761070   P - in nearby town WC ‖ ♿   🚂 - Weymouth

2 BRANKSOME CHINA WORKS

Shaftesbury Street, Fordingbridge, Hampshire

This fascinating working factory makes fine porcelain tableware. The works were started in 1945 by Ernest Baggaley, a skilled technical potter and designer who invented a unique fine porcelain and began making tableware to his own designs. The ware is very strong and durable and

is sold worldwide. The factory is still a family-run business. Open daily all year, except Sun. and Bank Holidays. ☎ 01425 652010

P WC ♿   🚂 - Salisbury

3 STAPEHILL ABBEY, CRAFTS & GARDENS

276 Wimborne Road West, near Wimborne, Dorset

Stapehill is really four attractions in one, and much of what's on offer is conveniently undercover. For 200 years, Stapehill was home to an order of Cistercian nuns. Today, it offers an adventure playground, farmyard, pony rides, abbey buildings and a stunning cloister garden, which is a haven of peace and tranquillity. Watch crafts-people at work or walk around the countryside displays. Open daily Feb.-Dec., except Christmas *(reduced hours in winter)*. ☎ 01202 861686

P WC ‖ ♿   🚂 - Bournemouth or Poole

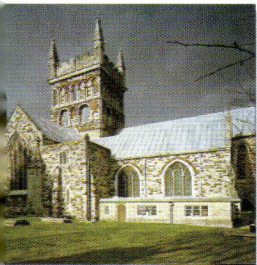

4 MINSTER CHURCH OF ST CUTHBERGA

High Street, Wimborne Minster, Dorset

The Minster Church of St Cuthberga was founded in the year 705, although the present church is mostly Norman with later additions. It is a magnificent building and dominates the area for miles around. It is not a museum and is still in use as a church, containing many interesting treasures, such as a 14th-century astronomical clock. There is also a well-stocked shop. The town has a coach park and passengers can alight outside the Minster in King Street. Open daily *(restrictions during services)*.

P - in nearby town 🚾 🍴 ♿
🚌 - Bournemouth or Poole

5 POOLE POTTERY

The Quay, Poole, Dorset

Since 1873, Poole Pottery has been renowned worldwide for its innovative tableware. Over a million visitors each year come to see how the pottery is made, following this fascinating process from start to finish. As well as a factory tour, admission entitles you to visit the museum, cinema, Master Potter's Gameshow and a have-a-go at pottery area, two of

the many interactive displays for children. There is also a factory shop, tearoom and restaurant. Open daily all year, except Christmas Day.
☎ 01202 666200

P 🚾 🍴 ♿   🚌 - Poole

6 OCEANARIUM

Pier Approach, West Beach, Bournemouth

This new £3 million attraction is all undercover, housed in a stunning Art-Deco style building. Cleverly designed multi-level displays take you on a voyage of discovery around the world, from the Antarctic to the Great Barrier Reef. Travel from the Atlantic to the Caribbean and see live exhibits from four different continents, including stingrays, sharks and piranhas. Open daily all year, except Christmas Day. ☎ 01202 311993

P - nearby 🚾 🍴 ♿   🚌 - Bournemouth

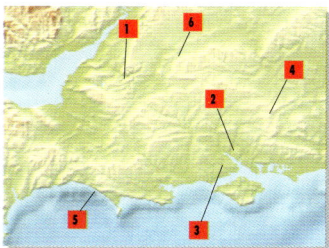

The following attractions are for those people who want just that little bit more from their holiday. Days of Adventure are action-packed, hands-on experiences which involve an element of physical exertion. From windsurfing to ballooning, these activities will satisfy anyone looking for a more energetic day out.

1 BALLOONING

One of the most unusual and exhilarating ways to see the countryside is from a hot-air balloon. There is something quite magical about the experience of drifting silently across the landscape at little more than walking pace. Balloon trips are usually made in the early morning or evening to take advantage of favourable wind conditions, and you never quite know where you will end up. Most passengers are invited to help inflate and deflate the balloon as part of the experience. Try Bath Balloon flights, Bath, Avon ☎ 01225 466888 or Adventure Balloons, Hartley Wintney, Hampshire ☎ 01252 844222

2 WINDSURFING

Like many water sports today, windsurfing is becoming extremely popular. Experienced windsurfers can carry out manoeuvres every bit as sophisticated as ordinary surfboarders. Exhilarating and fun, and guaranteed to liven up your day at the beach, there are several windsurfing centres

in the region offering board hire and lessons for beginners. Contact RYA Windsurfing, Romsey Road, Eastleigh, Hampshire ☎ 02380 627400

3 PONY-TREKKING

There are plenty of opportunities for pony-trekking in the South, particularly in the New Forest, where there are numerous riding stables. Many offer a range of hacks (hourly, half-day or all-day), while several also offer supervised lessons and rides for beginners. For details of pony-trekking and horse-riding in the New Forest area, ring The Old Barn at Dale Farm, Applemore Hill, Dibden, Hampshire ☎ 02380 843180

4 GLIDING

Gliding is becoming increasingly popular, and there is no better place to try out your skills than in the wide-open skies above Wiltshire, north Hampshire and Dorset. As well as being exhilarating, gliding is also amazingly relaxing as you float effortlessly above the landscape – don't forget to take your camera to capture the breathtaking panoramic views. There are several gliding centres in the area offering trial and pleasure flights. Try the Lasham Gliding Society, Alton, Hampshire ☎ 01256 384900

5 FOSSIL-HUNTING

The cliffs and beaches of Dorset are ideal for those who enjoy searching for fossils. Much of the coastline here is made up of soft, crumbling rocks which are a mixture of sandstone, limestone and chalk. These have been worn away by the incessant action of the sea, to reveal a treasure trove of fossils from the Earth's prehistoric past. Some of the fossils are as much as 200 million-years-old and include such creatures as starfish and shellfish, once found in the warm, tropical waters

that washed these shores. The most common fossils found are ammonites, an extinct mollusc resembling a giant snail. Occasionally, dinosaur remains are discovered. It is possible to find fossils in the fallen debris from rock slides on the beaches – but check the tides beforehand to avoid being cut off. In the interests of conservation, fossils should simply be observed and photographed rather than removed from the site.

6 HANG-GLIDING

The cliffs of Dorset and the windswept hills of inland Dorset, Wiltshire and Hampshire are tailor-made for hang-gliding. There is no better way to see the countryside, flying as free as a bird on thermals. There are several places in the area offering lessons or trial flights. Try the A4 Hang-gliding & Paragliding School, Old Yatesbury Airfield, Yatesbury, Calne, Wiltshire ☎ 01672 861555

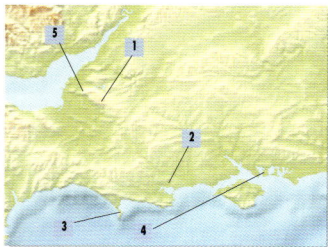

Those in search of an attraction with a little difference should find something to suit them on these pages. From a fascinating glimpse into Britain's great maritime history to the exploration of ancient caves, there's plenty to choose from to make an unusual and enjoyable day out.

1 WOOKEY HOLE CAVES

Wookey Hole, Wells, Somerset

These spectacular caves were carved out by the River Axe, resulting in caverns which penetrate deep into the Mendip Hills. Visitors can enjoy a tour through the best of these caverns, including the enormous Cathedral Cave which is brought to life by a sound and light show. You can also discover the source of the mysterious River Axe as it emerges from underground. A fascinating museum traces 50,000 years of human history and legend, while the Wookey Hole Paper Mill shows the ancient craft of papermaking in action. Children will particularly enjoy the undercover pier which has a wealth of traditional seaside entertainment. Open daily all year, except 17-25 Dec. ☎ 01749 672243

P WC ●| / & except for caves 🚆 - Bristol Temple-Meads & Weston-super-Mare

2 POOLE AQUARIUM & SERPENTARIUM

Hemmings Wharf, The Quay, Poole, Dorset

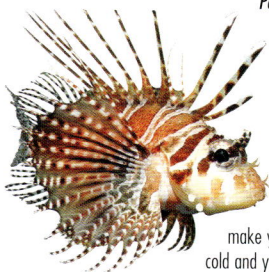

Not for the faint-hearted, the Poole Aquarium & Serpentarium specializes in all those creatures that make your blood run cold and your skin crawl! The complex is full of amazing animals, from black-tip sharks and piranhas, to bird-eating spiders, crocodiles and snakes...lots of them! The centre has been highly praised for its educational programmes and the high standard of care enjoyed by the animals. Open daily all year, except Christmas Day. ☎ 01202 686712

P - nearby WC ●| & 🚆 - Poole

3 PORTLAND BILL

Dorset (follow signs off the A354)

The Isle of Portland lies at the southern extremity of Dorset, separated from the mainland only by a narrow neck of land, part of the famous Chesil Beach, a giant ridge of shingle (see page 6). At the southern end of the isle lies Portland Bill, a rocky promontory jutting out into the Channel and crowned by a lighthouse. Seas can be ferocious here, but the landscape is very special. At times almost lunar in appearance, it is a haunting, atmospheric place. The massive walls of Portland's artificial harbour were built by convicts awaiting transportation in 1847.

P WC ●| & 🚆 - Weymouth

4 FLAGSHIP PORTSMOUTH

At the Historic Dockyard, Porter's Lodge,
Building 1/7 College Road, HM Naval Base, Portsmouth

Flagship Portsmouth is home to three of the world's greatest historic ships – *The Mary Rose*, *HMS Victory* and *HMS Warrior* (1860), the pride of Queen Victoria's fleet. The ships are set among historic Georgian buildings which house the new galleries and exhibitions of the Royal Naval Museum, including Horatio Nelson, the Hero and the Man, The Sailing Navy and the new Victory Gallery featuring Trafalgar and the Story of *HMS Victory*. Action Stations, a multimedia attraction, opens in autumn 2000. Visitors can also take a 'Warships by Water' harbour tour. Open daily all year, except Christmas Day. ☎ 02392 861512 *(info line)* or 02392 861533 *(other enquiries)*

P ⌨ ⵏ & 🚂 - Portsmouth Harbour

5 CHEDDAR CAVES & GORGE

Cheddar, Somerset

Famous for its beautiful stalagmite caves, Cheddar Gorge is a natural wilderness which stretches for 3 miles (4 km) through the heart of rural Somerset. Here England's highest inland cliffs offer visitors stunning views across the surrounding countryside, together with a chance to glimpse a rich variety of wildlife, including several rare species of butterflies and insects. The whole family will enjoy exploring the fascinating caves, including Gough's Cave which contains countless stalactites and stalagmites and stunning, cathedral-like caverns carved out by the meltwaters of the last Ice Age. Cox's Cave, though smaller, contains equally fantastic shapes and colours, all enhanced by sound, lighting and special effects. There are a wealth of other attractions, including bus tours of the gorge, shops selling the work of artists and local craftspeople, plus the Crystal Quest (a children's fantasy adventure). For the more energetic, there are half-day introductions to caving, climbing and abseiling. Open daily, except 24-25 Dec. ☎ 01934 742343

P ⌨ ⵏ & (limited) 🚂 - Weston-super-Mare

ANCIENT CAPITAL

Until the 9th century, Britain was a divided land with many separate kingdoms. In 802, Ecgberht, King of Wessex, became recognized as the first king of all England, but peace did not last. It took the strong rule of King Alfred (known as The Great) to finally unite the Saxons. He made Winchester the capital of England, and it became the most important city in the land. After the Norman Conquest, the seat of government was gradually moved to London, although Winchester remained an important royal town throughout the Middle Ages.

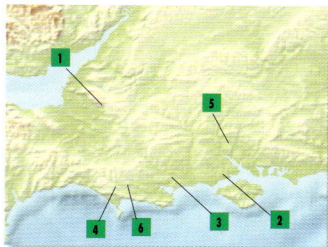

In this section you will find some of the surprises of the South – some already well-known, others not so familiar. But all have something special, or unusual, to offer the visitor who has more time to hunt them out. Choose from ancient stone circles to scenic rural villages that conjure up life long ago.

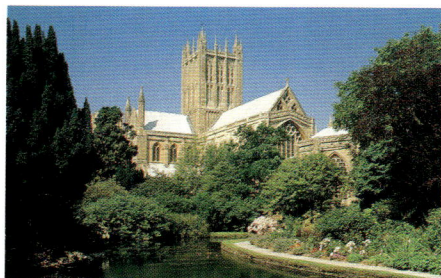

1 WELLS

Somerset

The small, ancient city of Wells is a delight and gives a truer picture than most of what a medieval city might have looked like. It is dominated by its cathedral, one of the smallest in Britain, but also one of the most architecturally splendid. The building dates from the late 12th century, but has many additions. Adjacent is the moated and fortified Bishop's Palace and the Vicar's Close, a remarkable street of 14th-century houses. The town is a warren of narrow streets lined with many fine medieval buildings.

P WC ⦿ & 🚌 - Bridgwater

2 BUCKLER'S HARD

Near Beaulieu, Hampshire

Located in the southeastern corner of the New Forest, Buckler's Hard is one of the most historic and scenically beautiful parts of the region. The village consists of little more than an elegant street of quaint houses, with an open expanse running gently down to the River Beaulieu. Yachts

and pleasure craft are moored in the small quay now, but it was a major ship-building centre in Tudor and Georgian times. There is a maritime museum, as well as river cruises in summer and plenty of peace and quiet. *Note that cars are not permitted in the centre.*

P WC ⦿ & 🚌 - Lymington

3 PRIEST'S HOUSE, MUSEUM & GARDEN

23-27 High Street, Wimborne, Dorset

The Priest's House is, rather unusually, housed in what was once an ironmonger's shop in the High Street. It contains many fascinating local history exhibits in a delightful, authentic setting. The house dates from the 16th century, and outside is a charming walled garden. Many children's events and hands-on displays are featured on a regular basis. Open Mon.-Sat., Apr.-Oct. (plus Sun., Jun.-Sept.); also Bank Holiday weekends (afternoons only).

📞 01202 882533 P WC ⦿ & 🚌 - Bournemouth or Poole

4 CERNE ABBAS GIANT

East of Cerne Abbas village (off the A352), Dorset

As fertility symbols go, you won't find many bigger than this! The Cerne Abbas Giant is a 180-ft (60-metre) high figure of a naked man, complete with club, which is believed to have been carved into the chalk of this Dorset hillside about 1,500 years ago, perhaps earlier. Its true purpose remains a mystery, although it was probably some sort of message to an ancient fertility god. Even up to the last century, some barren women believed that sleeping on the giant would make them fertile. Now protected by the National Trust, the giant can be freely seen from the road to Cerne Abbas village, from where a footpath gives access to the giant itself.

P & ☎ - Dorchester

5 KING JOHN'S HOUSE

Church Street, Romsey

This little gem lay virtually undiscovered until 1927, when a local historian realized that it was one of the oldest surviving inhabited houses in England. It also contains a rare and somewhat macabre feature — a floor made from pieces of animal bone. In 1306, the house was used by members of King Edward I's retinue, who scratched graffiti into the plaster. There are several

permanent displays inside the house and a restored period garden to the rear. Open daily, Easter-Sept. ☎ 01794 512200

WC & (ground floor only) ☎ - Romsey

6 MILTON ABBAS

Dorset

This is another delightful village in which Dorset seems to specialize, made up of a long main street of thatched cottages which seem hardly to have changed for centuries. Dominated by its 14th-century abbey church, the village preserves an old-world charm and makes an ideal touring base from which to visit the unspoilt Dorset countryside.

P WC ⍭ & ☎ - Wareham

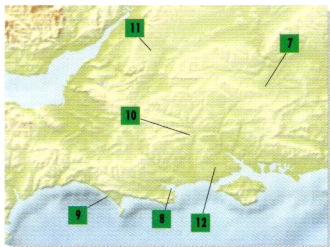

7 BASINGSTOKE CANAL VISITORS' CENTRE

Mytchett Place Road, Mytchett, near Camberley, Surrey

Discover the wonderful world of narrow boats, barges and canals in an attractive setting. There are towpath walks, nature trails and picnic areas, an exhibition and summer boat trips (at weekends and school holidays), a day-hire boat (book in advance) and a café. In all, a pleasant, relaxing day out. Open all year, Tues.-Sun. plus Bank Holiday Mondays, Easter-Sept., and Tues.-Fri., Oct.-Easter. ☎ 01252 370073

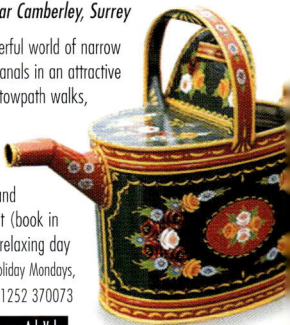

P WC ॥◎। & 🚉 - North Camp or Ash Vale

8 BROWNSEA ISLAND

Poole Harbour, Dorset

Brownsea Island was once privately owned and run almost as a miniature feudal state by its eccentric owners, who were keen to preserve the island's unique character. Brownsea, sitting right at the heart of Poole Harbour, is now owned and protected by the National Trust. Some 500 acres (200 hectares) in area, the island has a variety of habitats, from woodland and heath to quiet beaches (safe for bathing) and rocky shores. A large part of the island is now a nature reserve. Open daily, Mar.-Sept. Regular passenger ferries operate from Poole Harbour, a limited ferry service runs from Bournemouth and Swanage. ☎ 01202 707744

P WC ॥◎। & 🚉 - Poole

9 ABBOTSBURY

Dorset

This beautiful village in Dorset has a very long main street, containing many thatched cottages and one of the longest tithe barns in England, measuring 276 ft (84 metres). This 15th-century barn is the last remnant of the village's Benedictine abbey. The monks established a swannery here to provide birds for their table. Today the swannery is home to over 600 free-flying swans and has become a favourite visitor attraction. There is an audiovisual

display, a children's Ugly Duckling Trail and shire-horse-and-cart rides. Swannery open daily, Easter -Oct. ☎ 01305 871130

P WC ॥◎। & 🚉 - Dorchester

10 ROCKBOURNE VILLAGE

Near Fordingbridge, Hampshire

At the far northwestern edge of the New Forest can be found the idyllic village of Rockbourne, considered by many to be the prettiest village in the forest — although there are several

contenders! With its charming thatched cottages nestled beside a stream in a quiet valley, this is traditional England. Nearby is the Rockbourne Roman Villa.

🅿 ♿ 🚌 - Salisbury

11 AVEBURY STONE CIRCLE

6 miles (10 km) west of Marlborough, Wiltshire (off the A4361)

At the northern extremity of the region lies Avebury, one of the most important prehistoric sites in Europe. The enormous stone circle here may lack the impressive architecture of Stonehenge, but it covers a much wider area and is more complex. In addition to the main circle there are several smaller ones, together with stone avenues and processional ways, and Silbury Hill, all dating from about 2500 BC, and providing evidence of a sophisticated society at that time. The true purpose of the monuments will perhaps always remain a mystery. The village of Avebury is situated within part of the main circle. The site is freely accessible at any time 📞 01672 539250

🅿 🚾 🍴 ♿ 🚌 - Pewsey

12 LYNDHURST

Hampshire

Lyndhurst is usually regarded as the 'capital' of the New Forest, as it lies more-or-less at the heart of this area and is the seat of the Verderers' Court, the ancient administration body for the forest. It is a sizeable town with every modern facility and is home to the New Forest Musem (see page 30). Although often bypassed by visitors because of its size, it has many fascinating corners to explore and makes an ideal base from which to tour the forest. Mrs Hargreaves, formerly Alice Liddell and the model for Lewis Carroll's character Alice in Wonderland, is buried in the churchyard.

🅿 🚾 🍴 ♿ 🚌 - Lyndhurst

The New Forest, in Hampshire, covers more than 90,000 acres (36,400 hectares), with about two-thirds of the land open to the public. Thousands of visitors come for the tranquillity, the beautiful countryside and, of course, the ponies. Discover more about this beautiful area to help you get the most from your visit.

ORIGINS OF THE FOREST

Contrary to popular belief, the word 'forest' did not originally mean an area completely covered by trees. In medieval times, it simply meant an area set aside for hunting, and included woods and open land. After the Conquest, the Norman kings set aside huge areas of royal forest, exclusively for their own private hunting. The New Forest was designated as one of the first of these in 1079.

ECOLOGY OF THE FOREST

In Britain today, there remain only a few isolated pockets of virgin landscape which have been unaltered by humans in some way. It is doubtful if any of the New Forest is part of the original wildwood, the natural tree cover that once carpeted the land. The first woodland clearances began as long ago as the Bronze Age, perhaps earlier. These in turn created much of the scrub and heathland of the New Forest. The region is made up of a wide variety of landscapes, from open heath and grassland, to woodland cover (both deciduous and coniferous), which support a huge diversity of plant and animal life.

THE RUFUS STONE

One of the most celebrated spots in the New Forest is marked by a simple memorial known as the Rufus Stone. It marks the spot where William II (known as Rufus), William the Conqueror's son, was shot and killed by an arrow in 1100, supposedly in a hunting accident. A chance arrow, fired by one Walter Tyrell, glanced off a tree and struck the king. The circumstances of William's death have always been suspicious. He may have been assassinated, since his brother Henry, who was in the vicinity, seized the royal treasure at Winchester and had himself crowned king a few days later. The Rufus Stone is located on a signed road off the A31, 3 miles (5 km) southeast of Cadnam. It can be freely visited at any time.

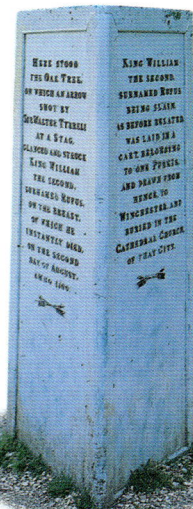

VISITING THE FOREST

Some eight million people visit the New Forest each year, but it is usually possible to escape the crowds and enjoy a huge variety of peaceful walks or rides. There are numerous car-free gravel roads throughout the forest, with signed trails in some parts for walkers or cyclists. Cars can be parked in the many clearings dotted around the forest, some of which have toilets. There are plenty of picnic sites to choose from, although you will generally need to take your own refreshments. (To find out more about the life and work of the forest, why not visit the New Forest Museum in Lyndhurst? You can find out the details for this on page 30.)

P WC 🚂 - Brockenhurst or Lyndhurst

NEW FOREST PONIES

In ancient times, wild ponies roamed freely over much of Britain. Today, a few semi-wild breeds still survive, such as the Dartmoor and New Forest ponies. For centuries, commoners have been allowed to let their cattle and ponies roam freely in the forest. Nowadays, most carry their owners' brand and many are rounded up each year for sale. The ponies are genuinely unafraid of traffic, and so visitors are forbidden to feed them to prevent accidents caused by ponies approaching cars. There is a strict speed limit for driving in and around the forest, but even so, there are cases of vehicles colliding with ponies. Visitors are advised to take great care, especially at night when it can be very difficult to see these animals, although some have fluorescent tags which show up in headlights.

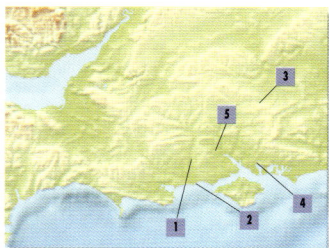

The South of England boasts some of the finest historic monuments in Britain, from the mysterious and gigantic stone circle at Stonehenge, to magnificent castles, cathedrals and stately homes. These fascinating places provide a key to Britain's rich and varied past, and all have plenty to satisfy the visitor's curiosity.

2 CHRISTCHURCH PRIORY

Quay Road, Christchurch, Dorset

Christchurch Priory comes as something of a surprise on this busy holiday coast of Dorset. First built in the 7th century, the priory was rebuilt by the Normans and contains examples of most architectural styles. The church is famed for its beauty and calm atmosphere. According to legend, while the church was being built, a mysterious carpenter came to work there. When a beam was

1 ROCKBOURNE ROMAN VILLA

Signposted from Rockbourne Village, Hampshire

Discovered by accident in 1942, the site of this important and extensive Roman villa has now been fully excavated. An attractive, modern museum displays many objects found at the site in a highly imaginative way. Of special interest are the visible remains of the hypocaust (underfloor heating system) and fine mosaics. Open daily, Apr.-Sept (and Easter, if in March); closed weekday mornings.
📞 01725 518541

🅿 ♿ 🚌 - Salisbury

mistakenly cut too short, the carpenter miraculously restored it to its proper length overnight. The town was renamed in honour of Christ and this miraculous beam. Open daily, except Christmas Day. 📞 01202 485804

🅿 🍽 ♿ 🚌 - Christchurch

3 BASING HOUSE

Redbridge Lane, Basing, near Basingstoke, Hampshire

Basing House was once reckoned to be the largest house in Elizabethan England — one wing alone was said to contain over 360 rooms. However, the house suffered a prolonged siege during the Civil War and gradually fell into disrepair. The ruins cover an area of 10 acres (4 hectares) and contain the earthworks of a Norman castle, parts of the Tudor palace and remnants of the Civil War defences. There is also a small exhibition of archaeological finds from the ruins. Open afternoons only, Wed.-Sun., plus Bank Holidays, Apr.-Sept. ☎ 01256 467294

P WC 🚌 - Basingstoke

LOCAL CHEESES

Britain has many specialist cheeses, most of them local to a specific area of the country. Originally, they were made by farmers' wives as an additional source of income. One of these local specialities is Dorset Blue Vinny (or Veiny). It is a variation of the Stilton-type cheese, made from hand-skimmed milk. It is usually eaten with another local speciality, Dorset knobs — small, round and very crispy bread rolls.

4 PORTCHESTER CASTLE

South of Portchester (off the A27), Fareham, Hampshire

Portchester Castle contains the most complete circuit of Roman walls in northern Europe. It began life as a fort on the Saxon shore, built by the Romans in c. AD 270 to repel Saxon pirates. In 1120, a medieval castle was built in one corner of the inner compound, the fort then acting as a huge outer bailey. In another corner of the fort, a priory was founded in 1133. The walls are impressive and afford fine views of Portsmouth and the Solent, especially from the top of the keep, which housed over 3,000 prisoners during the Napoleonic wars. There is much to see, including an interactive exhibition. Open daily all year, except 24-26 Dec. ☎ 02392 378291

P WC 🍴 ♿ - limited access 🚌 - Portchester

5 ROMSEY ABBEY

Church Street, Romsey, Hampshire

Founded in 907, the present church (Norman and Early English, 1120 −1240) is the third to occupy this site. In around 1532, the abbey was bought by the townspeople for £100 and has since served as the parish church of Romsey. There are important Saxon sculptures to be seen and some fine 16th-century painted panelling. It is also the burial place of Earl Mountbatten of Burma. The interior is beautiful and there are

many monastic remains. Guided tours are available. Open daily, all year. ☎ 01794 513125

P WC ♿ 🚌 - Romsey

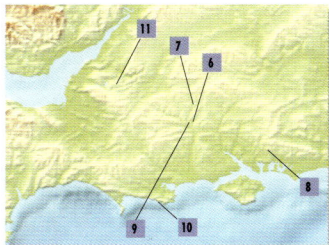

6 SALISBURY CATHEDRAL

Salisbury, Wiltshire

Salisbury is probably the finest medieval cathedral in Britain. It has the highest spire (404 ft/123 metres), the best preserved original copy of Magna Carta (1215), a unique 13th-century frieze of bible stories in the octagonal Chapter House, and Europe's oldest working clock (1386). Choristers sing daily services, continuing a tradition of worship that goes back over 750 years. Volunteers provide guided tours highlighting the cathedral's many treasures, including tours of the tower. Stonehenge and Old Sarum are also within easy reach of this area. Open daily, all year.

☎ 01722 555120 🅿 WC ⍾ & 🚃 - Salisbury

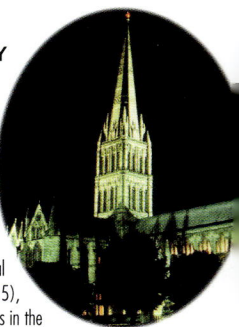

7 STONEHENGE

Salisbury Plain, Wiltshire, 2 miles (3 km) west of Amesbury (on the junction of the A303 and A344/A360)

The ancient stone circle of Stonehenge (English Heritage) is one of the wonders of the world, dating back to the great temples and pyramids of Egypt. Visitors over the centuries have tended to focus on the massive stones, but Stonehenge is not an isolated monument. It stands at the centre of an extensive prehistoric landscape, which is filled with the remains of ceremonial and domestic structures, some older than Stonehenge itself. Many of these features — earthworks, burial mounds and so on — are accessible by road or public footpath. Stonehenge and its surroundings remain powerful witness to the great civilizations of the Stone and Bronze ages, between 5,000 and 3,000 years ago. A free audio tour helps visitors to discover the history of this unique monument. Open daily, except 24-26 Dec.

☎ 01980 624715 (info line); 01980 626267 (to arrange private access)

🅿 WC ⍾ & 🚃 - Salisbury

8 UPPARK HOUSE

South Harting, near Petersfield, Hampshire

Uppark House (National Trust) stands high on the South Downs. Built in 1690, the elegant mid-18th-century interior has been fully restored following a disastrous fire in 1989. Included among the treasures are a fine collection of paintings, ceramics, textiles and furniture. There is also an award-winning multimedia exhibition detailing the impressive restoration

work. H G Wells spent part of his youth at Uppark when his mother was housekeeper there in 1880–92. Open Sun.-Thur, Apr.-Oct. ☎ 01730 825415 or 01730 825857 (info line)

🅿 WC ⍾ & 🚃 - Petersfield

9 WILTON HOUSE

3 miles (5 km) west of Salisbury,
(on the A30), Wiltshire

Wilton House is built on the site of a dissolved Benedictine Abbey. The present house was built between 1647–53 for the Earl of Pembroke. Inigo Jones designed the magnificent state rooms, including the renowned Double Cube Room. Surrounding the house are 21 acres (8 hectares)

of landscaped parkland, bordered by the River Nadder which is the setting for the majestic Palladian Bridge. The visitor centre's award-winning film, together with its Victorian Laundry and Tudor Kitchen, allows visitors to follow the history of the house and its inhabitants. There is also an adventure playground and gift shop. Open daily, Apr.-Oct.
☎ 01722 746729 *(info line)*

🅿 🚾 🍴 ♿ 🚍 - Salisbury

10 CORFE CASTLE

The Square, Corfe Castle, Dorset

The outstanding location of Corfe Castle, on a precipitous hill on the Isle of Purbeck, was made all the more austere by the Parliamentarians, who shattered the walls during two sieges in the Civil War. Many of the houses in the village at the foot of the hill were built from stone robbed from these walls. The castle was first built in the 11th century, and later additions include a keep and a palatial suite of rooms built for King John. There are magnificent views of Poole and the Isle of Wight from the top of the hill. Open daily, Mar.-Oct. *(reduced hours during winter months).* ☎ 01929 481294 or 01929 480609 *(visitor centre)*

🅿 🚾 🍴 🚍 - Wareham

11 ROMAN BATHS

Abbey Churchyard,
Bath, Somerset

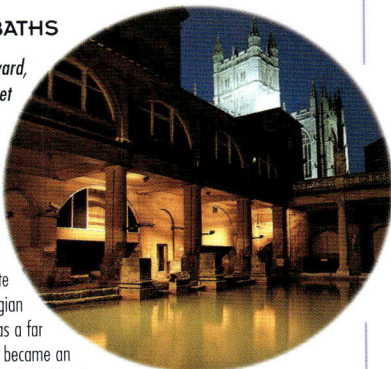

Although a little distant to the main area covered by this guide, we cannot recommend too highly a brief excursion to the magnificent city of Bath. Famed as the most complete and best-preserved Georgian town in Britain, it has a far older pedigree. The site became an important Roman settlement in AD 44 when a bath house was built around a spring that produced waters of medicinal renown. Much of the Roman baths remains, alongside the 18th-century pump room, built when the town became a fashionable spa. Open daily, all year. ☎ 01225 477785

🅿 🚾 🍴 ♿ 🚍 - Bath

Britain is famed for the beauty of its gardens which, collectively, contain a greater diversity of plants than any other place in the world. Visiting gardens has become a popular pastime and features strongly on many visitors' itineraries. Happily, the South offers an impressive range of horticultural delights.

1 RED HOUSE, MUSEUM & GARDENS

Quay Road, Christchurch, Dorset

Red House has a garden with a difference and a fascinating history. The house was built in 1763, originally as a parish workhouse. It was later converted, first into a private house and then into a private museum. It is now open to the public and features fine modern displays of archaeology, and local and national history and costumes. Surrounding the house is a peaceful and authentic garden, with many unusual varieties of plants, especially old varieties of roses, creating a unique atmosphere.

Open daily, Tues.-Sun. ☎ 01202 482860 P ❚❙❙ 🚂 - Christchurch

2 BOWOOD HOUSE & GARDEN

In Derry Hill Village (off the A4 midway between Calne and Chippenham), Wiltshire

Bowood is the magnificent family home of the Marquis and Marchioness of Lansdowne. It stands in glorious parkland, with gently sloping lawns stretching down to a lake. Also in the gardens are a beautiful cascading

waterfall, a Doric temple and terraced rose gardens. There is a separate area of stunning rhododendron gardens, which is open for six weeks during the flowering season from late April to early June. Another feature is the adventure playground. Open daily, Apr.-Oct. ☎ 01249 812102 *(info line)*

P ᴡᴄ ❚❙❙ ♿ 🚂 - Chippenham

3 KNOLL GARDENS & NURSERY

Stapehill Road, Hampreston, near Ferndown, Dorset

This place started in 1970 as Wimborne Botanic Gardens, on what was then a carrot field and area of scrub. The garden has since changed hands several times, each successive owner carrying out improvements and introducing new features. The gardens contain many special collections and are a joy to visit at any time of year. There is also an all-weather visitor centre. The garden makes an ideal venue for less mobile visitors and has a recommended wheelchair route. Open daily, Apr.-Oct.; Wed.-Sun. at other times. ☎ 01202 873931

P ᴡᴄ ❚❙❙ ♿ 🚂 - Bournemouth

4 THE VYNE, HOUSE & GARDEN

Sherborne St John (off the A340), Basingstoke, Hampshire

Originally built in the early 16th century for Lord Sandys (Henry VIII's Lord Chamberlain) and sold to Chaloner Chute, Speaker of the House of Commons in 1653, the estate was given to the National Trust by Sir Charles Chute in 1956. With its many alterations, it represents over 400 years of family life and history. Surrounding the house is magnificent 18th-century parkland. There are gardens, including an interesting Edwardian-style flower garden, and lawns sloping down to the lake. Open Tues.-Thur., Sat.& Sun., Apr.-Oct.

01256 881337 *(info line)*

P WC ▮ & 🚌 - Bramley

5 CRANBORNE MANOR & GARDEN

4 High Street, Cranborne, Wimborne, Dorset

This is a beautiful and historic garden surrounding an ancient manor house. It was laid out at the beginning of the 17th century by Mounten Jennings and John Tradescant. The garden has been much enlarged since then and now consists of walled gardens, yew

hedges, lawns, a wild garden with spring bulbs, herb garden, Jacobean mount garden, flowering cherries and a collection of old-fashioned roses. Alongside the garden is Cranborne Manor Garden Centre, which is open daily and sells a range of gardening products. It specializes in old-fashioned roses and herbs. Garden: open Wed., Mar.-Sept. 01725 517289

P WC ▮ & 🚌 - Salisbury or Bournemouth

SILBURY HILL

Close to the prehistoric stone circles and avenues at Avebury and West Kennett is the impressive Silbury Hill. At 130 ft (40 m) high and covering an area of over 5 acres (2 hectares), it is the largest prehistoric man-made mound in Europe. Although legend claims it is the gigantic burial mound of one King Sil, no ancient burial has ever been found within. It was carefully constructed of chalk blocks, but its purpose remains a mystery. *Please note that access to the hill itself is not permitted.*

6 FURZEY GARDENS

Minstead (off the A31), near Lyndhurst, Hampshire

The gardens at Furzey were first laid out in 1922 and opened to the public in 1930. Furzey House, built at the beginning of the 20th century, is probably the largest thatched house in the New Forest. Set in the picturesque village of Minstead, in the heart of the forest, its informal garden is renowned for its peace and tranquillity. There is a lake, heather garden and fernery, a craft centre and three play log cabins for younger visitors. Open daily, all year. 02380 812297 or 02380 812464 *(info line)*

P WC ▮ & 🚌 - Brockenhurst

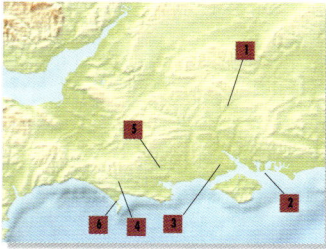

The museums of Southern England cover a fascinating range of subjects, with a bias towards naval history, inspired no doubt by the area's wealth of associations with the royal fleet. Included here are some of the region's more unusual museum collections, to intrigue adults and children alike.

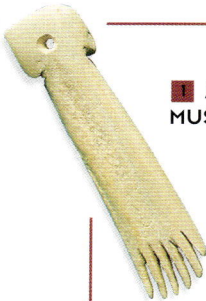

1 ANDOVER MUSEUM & MUSEUM OF THE IRON AGE

Church Close, Andover, Hampshire

These two museum collections are housed in buildings dating from c.1750, formerly a private residence which was later converted into a school. The Andover Museum covers local history, archaeology and natural history, while the Museum of the Iron Age specializes in finds made at Danebury Ring and other local hillforts, including both Roman and ancient British artefacts.

Open Tues.-Sat., all year. 01264 366283

🅿 ♿ 🍴 ♿   🚌 - Andover

2 D-DAY MUSEUM

Clarence Esplanade, Southsea, Hampshire

The D-Day Museum & Overlord Embroidery was opened by HRH the Queen Mother in 1984 to commemorate the 40th anniversary of the D-Day landings. The museum has proved enormously popular and has welcomed over 1.5 million visitors to see the internationally acclaimed embroidery and displays dedicated to Operation Overlord. It is the only museum in Britain devoted exclusively to World War II. Open daily all year, except 24-26 Dec.

 02392 827261   🅿 ♿ 🍴 ♿

🚌 - Portsmouth and Southsea

3 NEW FOREST MUSEUM

Main car park, High Street, Lyndhurst, Hampshire

The museum was established by a trust, whose main objectives are protecting and conserving the New Forest and educating the public in the life and work of the area. Visitors can see an audiovisual display, which gives a good

background and understanding of the region and the range of facilities on offer throughout the forest. There is also a fine New Forest reference library for public use. Open daily all year, except Christmas Day (reduced opening in winter). 02380 283914

🅿 ♿ ♿   🚌 - Ashurst

4 DINOSAUR MUSEUM

Icen Way, Dorchester, Dorset

The Dinosaur Museum has been designed with children in mind, to teach them about dinosaurs and the prehistoric past in a fun and exciting way. Recently voted Dorset's Family Attraction of the Year, the museum is unique, being the only one in Britain devoted exclusively to dinosaurs. Displays include fossils, skeletons and life-sized reconstructions, coupled with audiovisual and hands-on

computer displays. The museum has also twice been chosen as one of Britain's top hands-on experiences. Open daily, all year. ☎ 01305 269880

P - nearby ⚇ ♿ (partial access)
🚌 - Dorchester, South or West

5 ROYAL SIGNALS MUSEUM

Blandford Camp, Dorset

The Royal Signals Museum began as a private collection in the 1930s, but has now grown to be a large, nationally important museum and archive. The museum traces the history of military communications, science and technology from the Crimean to the Gulf wars, including displays on the World wars, Korea and the Falklands. There are also special displays on military intelligence, military vehicles and motorbikes, uniforms, equipment and the story of the Enigma code breakers, who were instrumental in defeating Hitler. Open Mon.-Fri., all year; plus Sat.-Sun., May-Sept. ☎ 01258 482248

P ⚇ 🍴 ♿ 🚌 - Salisbury

6 PORTLAND MUSEUM

217 Wakeham, Portland, Dorset

The museum is housed in two picturesque thatched cottages high above Church Ope Cove, which inspired Thomas Hardy's novel *The Well Beloved*. The museum covers such topics as local history, shipwrecks, smuggling and quarrying. Outside is a sheltered garden, an ideal place to sit and reflect, or enjoy a picnic. There is also a talking museum for the visually impaired. Open Fri.-Tues., Apr.-Oct. ☎ 01305 821804

P ⚇ 🚌 - Weymouth

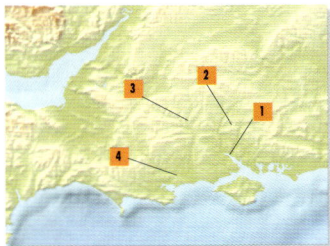

The South of England possesses some of the finest and most elegant historic towns in the country. These towns offer the visitor every conceivable form of attraction and service, with excellent shopping, hotel and restaurant facilities. Those listed here have been specially chosen with the visitor in mind.

1 SOUTHAMPTON

Southampton, in Hampshire, has long been famous as a major seaport, enjoying a unique double tide because of its position at the head of the Solent, which prolongs high water. Before the advent of modern air travel, Southampton was the main port of embarkation for passenger liners – in its heyday, it could berth up to eight liners at once. It is still a busy, thriving port which has adapted well to changing needs. At its centre is a bustling commercial city with excellent entertainment venues, fine restaurants and good shopping facilities. Much of the town centre was rebuilt following air raids in World War II, but substantial parts of the old town still survive, including some of the best-preserved medieval town walls in Britain.

P WC ۱O١ & 🚌 - Southampton

2 WINCHESTER

The ancient city of Winchester, in Hampshire, was made the capital of Wessex in 871 by Alfred the Great. After the Conquest in 1066, the Norman kings gradually moved their centre of government to London, but Winchester remained an important medieval city. The magnificent cathedral (the longest in Britain) still dominates the city centre. Several of the city gates also survive, along with the great hall of the castle, which contains a representation of King Arthur's legendary Round Table. There is a rich diversity of architectural styles and a graceful, well-proportioned high street, offering excellent shopping and restaurant facilities. Looking down on it all is an impressive statue of King Alfred. He would be proud of the place today, which is a vibrant and lively modern city, but which still preserves the best of its past.

P WC ۱O١ & 🚌 - Winchester

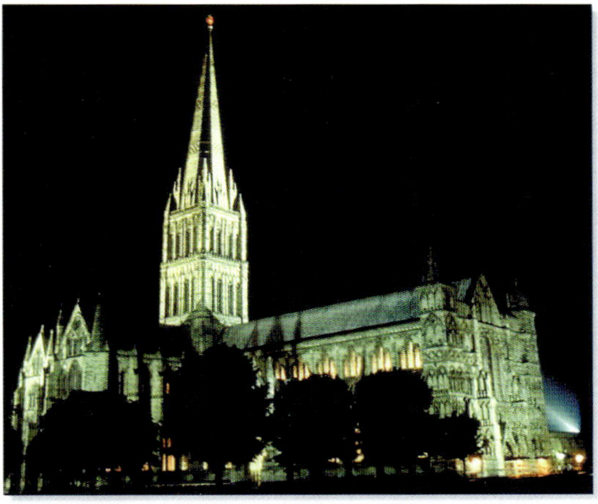

3 SALISBURY

Unlike many towns in Britain, which grew gradually from obscure beginnings, the foundation of Salisbury, in Wiltshire, can be precisely dated to 1220. In that year, Bishop Richard Poore decided to abandon the ancient, fortified city of Old Sarum, because of a poor water supply, and founded a new cathedral site 2 miles (3 km) south at a point where four river valleys met. The site became known as New Sarum, or Salisbury, and very soon an impressive town grew up around it. Old Sarum is now a deserted ruin. Salisbury continues to prosper today, and is a lively and spacious place, still surrounded by the water meadows that caused the new town to be built in the first place.

P WC - Salisbury

4 WIMBORNE MINSTER

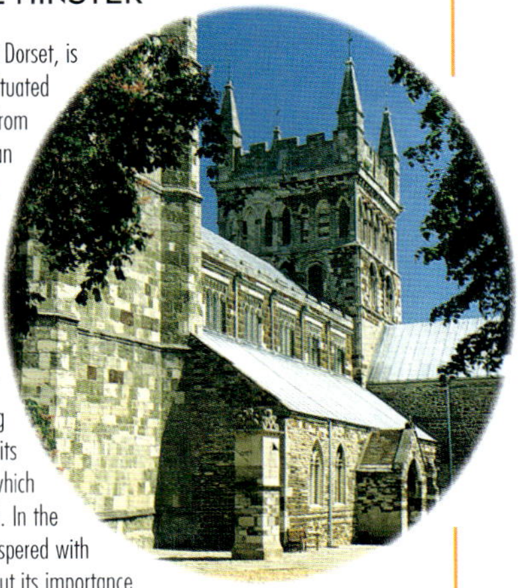

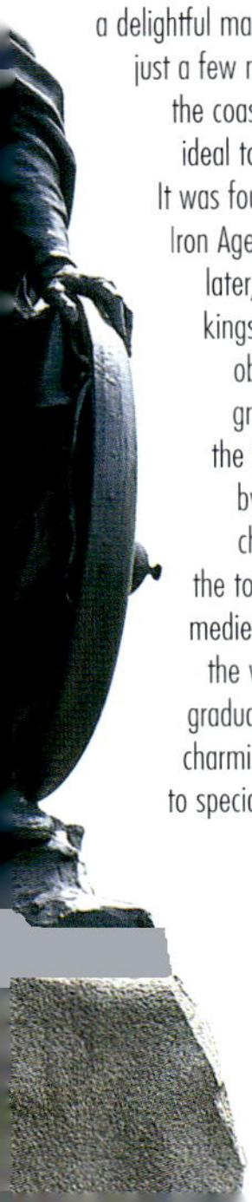

Wimborne Minster, in east Dorset, is a delightful market town. Situated just a few miles inland from the coast, it makes an ideal touring centre. It was founded in the Iron Age, and much later, the Saxon kings of Wessex obviously had great plans for the town, judging by the size of its church, after which the town is named. In the medieval era it prospered with the wool trade, but its importance gradually waned. Nowadays, it is one of those charming and atmospheric small market towns in which England seems to specialize. It also offers a wide range of shopping and visitor facilities.

P WC - Poole

ST SWITHIN'S DAY

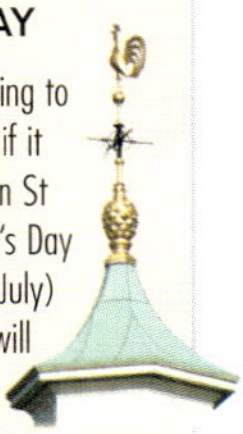

According to legend, if it rains on St Swithin's Day (15th July) then it will rain for the next 40 days. St Swithin was a Saxon bishop of Winchester and when he died in 862 the cathedral was dedicated in his name. He was buried outside the cathedral, as he had wished, but his body was later exhumed and placed inside the cathedral in a tomb more befitting a saint. This act is said to have so displeased the saint that it rained for 40 days after the event.

5 LYMINGTON

Lymington lies at the mouth of the Solent in Hampshire, where the River Lymington meets the sea. It once rivalled Southampton as one of Britain's premier ports, but today it is a lively sailing centre. Lying just a few miles south of the New Forest, it has become an important shopping and commercial centre for the area and makes an ideal base from which to explore the coast and forest. There is also a regular ferry (with the shortest crossing time of just half an hour) to the Isle of Wight.

P WC ❙❙ & 🚌 - Lymington

6 PORTSMOUTH

Portsmouth's fame and prosperity really began with the Tudors (although the town is far older), when Henry VIII began to use its sheltered harbour as a safe haven for his navy. The Royal Dockyard that grew up around the harbour firmly established the importance of the port, although this has declined somewhat in recent years. Portsmouth is an unselfconscious, workaday town, with few pretensions of grandeur. Unfortunately, it was a prime target during World War II and suffered much damage. Since then, some of the rebuilding has been uninspired, to say the least. However, much of old Portsmouth still survives, in pockets, and the docks area is a fascinating place to visit. Charles Dickens was born here in 1812.

P WC ❙❙ & 🚌 - Portsmouth

7 POOLE

Although Poole is Dorset's largest town, the area around the harbour remains remarkably unspoilt by modern development. The natural harbour is almost landlocked and measures an incredible 60 miles (97 km) around. It is reckoned to be the second largest natural harbour in the world, after Sydney in Australia. The old town built around the harbour has many nooks and crannies to explore, with numerous old inns and quaint streets. Modern Poole is a bustling town, with activities still largely centred on the sea front, offering all manner of visitor facilities. Brownsea Island (National Trust) sits at the heart of Poole Harbour and is now a nature reserve which can be visited by ferry (see page 20).

P WC ⦿ & | 🚌 - Poole

8 BOURNEMOUTH

Now almost continuous with Poole, and spreading eastwards along the coast from it for several miles, Bournemouth has become the premier resort town on the south coast. Much of the town is given over to tasteful housing and a large proportion of the population is of retirement age. This gives the place an air of gentility, but this is by no means the entire picture. Bournemouth is a seaside resort par excellence, with first-class entertainment venues featuring international stars, local and international symphony orchestras, plus every conceivable holiday attraction. The shopping here is probably the best on the South coast.

P WC ⦿ & | 🚌 - Bournemouth

*These two pages provide information about a selection
of events and festivals held on a regular basis in the
South of England throughout the year. Each entry
is listed by month and includes brief details. Although
most of these events are held annually, the exact dates
vary from year to year, in order to fall on convenient
weekends or public holidays. For this reason, specific dates
are not listed here. Instead, you are advised to contact the nearest local
Tourist Information Centre (see page 42) to find out the exact dates, plus
information on times and admission prices or details of any one-off events.*

APRIL/MAY

BATH SPRING FLOWER SHOW
Royal Victoria Park, Bath. *Major floral and horticultural show -
stalls, food, farming exhibitions, crafts and band concerts.*
☎ 01225 396021

NORTH SOMERSET SHOW
Ashton Court, Bristol. *Major agricultural show - farming displays,
stalls, horticulture, ring events.*
☎ 01179 643498

SAILORS' HOBBY HORSE, MINEHEAD
Minehead, Somerset. *Traditional
customs on or close to May Day -
dancing and street entertainment.*
☎ 01643 702087

MAY

BADMINTON HORSE TRIALS
Badminton, Avon. *World-famous
international equestrian event -
dressage, cross-country and showjumping.*
☎ 01454 218375

BLANDFORD GEORGIAN FAIR
Blandford, Dorset. *Celebration of the town's Georgian heritage -
crafts, funfairs, street entertainment and morris dancing.*
☎ 01258 480808

VINTAGE MOTORCYCLE RALLY
Weymouth sea front, Dorset. *Motorcycle parades and static displays.*
☎ 01305 785747 *(Tourist Information Centre)*

WEYMOUTH INTERNATIONAL BEACH KITE FESTIVAL
Weymouth beach, Dorset. *Britain's biggest kite-flying festival -
workshops, displays and fireworks.*
☎ 01305 785747 *(Tourist Information Centre)*

WEYMOUTH OYSTER FESTIVAL
Olde Harbour, Weymouth, Dorset. *Traditional harbourside festival -
street entertainment, funfair, side shows and oysters in plentiful supply.*
☎ 01305 785747 *(Tourist Information Centre)*

JUNE

GLASTONBURY PILGRIMAGE
Glastonbury, Somerset. *Annual Anglican pilgrimage through the town's streets.*
☎ 01179 568539

JULY

FARNBOROUGH INTERNATIONAL AIR SHOW
Farnborough Aerodrome, Hampshire. *One of the world's top air shows - static and flying displays, exhibitors, flight simulators and virtual reality flying with interactive games.*
☎ 0207 227 1043

NETLEY MARSH STEAM ENGINE RALLY
Netley Marsh, near Southampton, Hampshire. *Steam traction engines, crafts, farm machinery and displays.*
☎ 02380 867882

NEW FOREST & HAMPSHIRE COUNTY SHOW
New Park Showground, Brockenhurst, Hampshire. *Major agricultural and equestrian event - livestock, showjumping, exhibitions, stalls, arena events.*
☎ 01590 622400

PUDDLETOWN CARNIVAL
Puddletown, Dorset. *Carnival through the village streets - floats, procession and arena events.*
☎ 01305 848470

TOLPUDDLE RALLY
Tolpuddle village, near Dorchester, Dorset. *Premier rally for workers' movement in the South, in memory of the 'martyrs' - parades, speeches, stalls, wreath-laying ceremony, music and drama.*
☎ 01179 506425

AUGUST

LYME REGIS REGATTA & CARNIVAL
Lyme Regis and Uplyme, Dorset. *Colourful festival featuring maritime and carnival events, processions and street entertainment.*
☎ 01297 443933

WEYMOUTH CARNIVAL
Weymouth sea front, Dorset. *Traditional street carnival and procession.*
☎ 01305 785747 *(Tourist Information Centre)*

SEPTEMBER

MIDDLE WALLOP INTERNATIONAL AIR SHOW
Stockbridge, Hampshire. *Major international air show, held at the largest operational grass air field in Europe - air displays, static exhibitions, stalls, sideshows.*
☎ 01980 674461

SOUTHAMPTON INTERNATIONAL BOAT SHOW
Western Esplanade, Southampton. *The world's largest on-water boat show, covering all aspects of the boating industry.*
☎ 01784 473377

NOVEMBER

WEYMOUTH GUY FAWKES CELEBRATIONS
Weymouth sea front, Dorset. *Major firework display, giant beach bonfire, funfair and water sport record attempts.*
☎ 01305 785747 *(Tourist Information Centre)*

All of the larger towns, and most of the smaller ones, have an excellent selection of shops to suit all tastes, including the main high street chains. To make your stay in the South even more memorable, however, we have selected a range of specialist shops that cater for the more discerning, with an eye for the unusual.

ART & CRAFT SHOPS

Art and craft shops are ever popular with visitors wishing to find souvenirs of their stay in the South. Below are a few suggested places; some specialize in items made locally, so you can hunt down something a little more unusual.

BASINGSTOKE
Viables Craft Centre
Harrow Way
☎ 01256 473634
(A variety of crafts sold in a dozen or so different units.)

CHRISTCHURCH
The National Trust Gift Shop
18 Bridge Street
☎ 01202 490478

Ye Olde Eight Bells Shop
(Twynham Craft & Haberdashery)
16 Church Street
☎ 01202 470587
(Art and craft materials, gift ideas, tapestry.)

CORFE MULLEN
Turning Over
160 Springdale Road
☎ 01202 601483
(Decorative, turned wood goods. Visitors by appointment only.)

DORCHESTER
The National Trust Gift Shop
65 High West Street
☎ 01305 267535

POOLE
Merlin's Handicrafts
422 Ashley Road
☎ 01202 745418
(Comprehensive range of art and craft materials and gifts.)

SOUTHSEA
Hiscock Gallery
11 Stanley Street
☎ 02392 825330
(Artists' materials and gifts, local scenery watercolours and prints.)

WINCHESTER
Complete Artist
102 Crane Street
☎ 01722 335928
(Art and craft materials, gift ideas.)

CHINA, GLASS & GIFTWARE

The following is a small selection of gift shops offering exclusive items, from ethnic jewellery and clothes to fine glass and china.

BOURNEMOUTH
Carousel Gifts
20 Westbourne Arcade
☎ 01202 761166
(Many branded gift ideas, including Enchantica, Cherished Teds, Eggberts.)

POOLE
Master Plaster Casters
(At Poole Pottery)
East Quay Road
☎ 01202 685529
(Handmade plaster cottages and other models, ready to paint.)

RINGWOOD
China Studio
2 High Street
☎ 01425 475487
(Fine selection of quality china, porcelain and crystal.)

SALISBURY
Fisherton Mill
Design and Contemporary Craft Emporium
108 Fisherton Street
☎ 01722 415121
(Outdoor seasonal exhibition area, studio workshops, fine art, toys.)

Watsons
8-9 Queen Street
☎ 01722 320311
(One of finest selections of china, crystal and giftware in the South.)

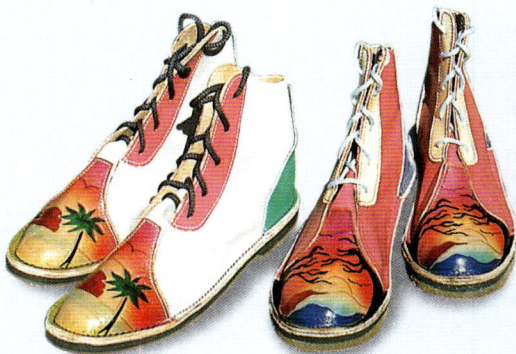

WEYMOUTH
La Luna
45 St Mary Street
☎ 01305 766936
(Handmade glassware and unique gifts.)

WILTON
The Wilton Shopping Village
Minster Street
☎ 01722 741211
(Wide variety of factory outlet shops, including fashion, textiles, glassware, golf equipment, china and so on, all at large discounts.)

ANTIQUES

There are many antique shops tucked away among the towns and villages of the South, but visitors who are on a tighter time limit may find these establishments of interest.

DORCHESTER
The Antiques Emporium
9 High East Street
☎ 01305 261546

RINGWOOD
R Morgan Antiques
90 Christchurch Road
☎ 01425 479400

WINCHESTER
Winchester Antiques
20A Jewry Street
☎ 01962 850123

MARKETS

Markets are always fun to explore and give the visitor a real flavour of the region. The following markets have been selected for their overall interest value, offering a range of items - from food, clothing and household goods to gifts, souvenirs and specialist goods. For full details of location, etc., contact the relevant local Tourist Information Centre (see page 42). Remember that the days on which markets are held can change. To avoid disappointment, it is always best to check beforehand.

Aldershot - *Thur.*
Alton - *Tues.*
Andover - *Thur. & Sat.*
Basingstoke - *Wed. & Sat.*
Dorchester - *Wed.*
Eastleigh - *Thur. & Sat.*
Fareham - *Mon.*
Fleet - *Sat.*
Gosport - *Tues. & Sat.*
Lymington - *Sat.*
Petersfield - *Wed. & Sat.*
Portsmouth - *Thur., Fri. & Sat.*
Ringwood - *Wed.*
Romsey - *Fri. & Sat.*
Salisbury - *Tues. & Sat.*
Southampton - *Tues. & Thur.-Sat.*
Weymouth - *Thur.*
Wimborne - *Fri., Sat. & Sun.*
Winchester - *Wed.-Sat.*

SHOPPING CENTRES

The following selection of undercover shopping centres and malls are ideal for shopping in any weather.

BOSCOMBE
Sovereign Centre
600 Christchurch Road

BOURNEMOUTH
Allen J J Shopping
Old Christchurch Road

The Avenue Shopping Centre
11-21 Commercial Road

CHRISTCHURCH
The Saxon Square Shopping Centre
Fareham town centre

FARNBOROUGH
The Kingsmead Shopping Centre
The Princes Mead

FLEET
The Hart Shopping Centre

POOLE
The Dolphin Shopping Centre
Kingland Road

PORTSMOUTH
The Bridge Shopping Centre

RINGWOOD
The Furlong Shopping Centre

SALISBURY
Cross Keys Shopping Centre
Market Square

The following information is provided to help visitors make the most of their stay in the South of England. None of the lists claims to be exhaustive (space precludes us from listing all the available details), but this selection of the more important information should provide a useful starting point.

WINING & DINING

The choice of eating establishments in the South is limitless. Every town and many villages boast a range of pubs, cafés and restaurants, some specializing in delicious local recipes. Most places in the area cater well for visitors, offering refreshments ranging from simple snacks to full restaurant meals. For that special occasion, however, the following restaurants have been singled out because of the excellence and good value of their cuisine. There are many others to try, of course, so why not seek these out for yourself in addition to using this guide to what's on offer.

BOURNEMOUTH
Bournemouth Steak House
208 Holdenhurst Road
📞 01202 293685

Trawlers Restaurant
42c Sea Road, Boscombe Spa
📞 01202 309238

CHRISTCHURCH
The Crooked Beam Restaurant
2 The Grove
📞 01202 499362

DORCHESTER
The Manor Hotel
Beach Road,
West Bexington
📞 01305 897616

Royal Oak
20 High West Street
📞 01305 262423

FERNDOWN
St Leonard's Hotel
185 Ringwood Road
📞 01425 471220

LOWER WOODFORD
The Wheatsheaf
📞 01722 782203

LYMINGTON
Harpers Bar Café
Kings Salterns Road
📞 01590 679971

Towle's Country Restaurant
Walhampton Hill
📞 01590 673113

MILTON ABBAS
The Tea Clipper Restaurant
The Street
📞 01258 880223

POOLE
Corkers Restaurant & Café Bar
1 High Street, Poole Quay
📞 01202 681393

WHITCHURCH
Woodlings Vineyard & Restaurant
📞 01256 895200

PORTLAND
The Stanley House Bistro
28 Easton Street
📞 01305 824022

RINGWOOD
Candlesticks Restaurant & Lodge
136 Christchurch Road
📞 01425 472587

SOUTHSEA
Fatty Arbuckles American Diner
Osborne Road
📞 02380 739179

WAREHAM
Kemps Country House Hotel & Restaurant
East Stoke
📞 01929 462563

WILTON
The Village Restaurant
Wilton Shopping Centre
King Street
📞 01722 741289

WHERE TO DRINK

Britain is famed for the number and variety of its inns and pubs. Many pubs now offer a range of services and facilities, including accommodation, entertainment and meals to suit all tastes. Increasingly, more pubs also serve a variety of real ales and fine wines. The following list of establishments is only a small selection, but each place is representative of the area in some way. The real joy of visiting pubs in any region of Britain, of course, is hunting out your own particular favourites from the huge variety available, but this list offers some useful suggestions.

BLANDFORD
The Cricketers
Shoton, Iwerne Courtney
📞 01258 860421

DORCHESTER
The Wise Man
West Stafford
📞 01305 263694

ILMINSTER
Perry's Cider Mills
Dowlish Wake
📞 01460 52681

MORETON
The Frampton Arms
Hurst Road
📞 01305 852253

POWERSTOCK
The Marquis of Lorne
Nettlecombe
📞 01308 485236

SALISBURY
The George and Dragon
85 Castle Street
📞 01722 333942

The New Inn and Old House Restaurant
New Street
📞 01722 327679

SHAFTESBURY
La Fleur de Lys
25 Salisbury Street
📞 01747 853717

SOUTHSEA
The Frog on the Front
Clarence Esplanade
☎ 02392 799977

STUCKTON
The Three Lions
Near Fordingbridge
☎ 01425 652489

WEST LULWORTH
The Castle Inn
☎ 01929 400311

WOODFALLS
The Woodfalls Inn
The Ridge
☎ 01725 513222

THEATRES

BLANDFORD
Bryanston Arts Centre
Blandford Forum
☎ 01258 456533

BOURNEMOUTH
Bournemouth International Centre
(Pavilion, Pier and Winter Gardens), Exeter Road
☎ 01202 456400

CHRISTCHURCH
Regent Centre
51 High Street
☎ 01202 499148

NEW MILTON
Forest Arts Centre
Old Milton Road
☎ 01425 612393

PORTLAND
Royal Manor Theatre Co.
138a Fortuneswell
☎ 01305 860792

PORTSMOUTH
New Theatre Royal
20-24 Guildhall Walk
☎ 02380 649000

ROMSEY
Plaza Theatre
Winchester Road
☎ 01794 523054

SALISBURY
Playhouse
Malthouse Lane
☎ 01722 320117

SHAFTESBURY
Shaftesbury Arts Centre
13 Bell Street
☎ 01747 854321

SOUTHAMPTON
The Guildhall
Civic Centre,
Havelock Road
☎ 02380 632601

Nuffield Theatre
University Road
☎ 02380 671771

SOUTHSEA
King's Theatre
Albert Road
☎ 01705 828282

SWANAGE
The Mowlem
Shore Road
☎ 01929 422229

WEYMOUTH
Pavilion Theatre and Ocean Room
The Esplanade
☎ 01305 783225

WINCHESTER
Theatre Royal
Jewry Street
☎ 01962 820220

CINEMAS

BOURNEMOUTH
ABC & MGM Cinemas
27 Westover Road
☎ (ABC) 01202 290345
☎ (MGM) 01202 558433

Odeon
Westover Road
☎ 01202 551086 /
08705 050007

CHRISTCHURCH
Regent Cinema
51 High Street
☎ 01202 479819 / 499148

DORCHESTER
Plaza Cinema
32 Trinity Street
☎ 01305 262488

POOLE
UCI
Tower Park
☎ 0990 888990

WAREHAM
Rex Cinemas
14 West Street
☎ 01929 552778

WEYMOUTH
Picturedrome
Gloucester Street
☎ 01305 785847

NIGHTCLUBS

BLANDFORD
G-Spot
8 Sunrise, Higher Shaftesbury Road
☎ 01258 459997

BOURNEMOUTH
Bla Bla
156-8 Old Christchurch Road
☎ 01202 295486

Bumbles Night Club
45 Poole Hill
☎ 01202 557006

Triangle Night Club
30 The Triangle
☎ 01202 297607

DORCHESTER
Paul's Night Club & Restaurant
33 Trinity Street
☎ 01305 268235

POOLE
Woody's Members Night Club
Aquarium Complex,
The Quay
☎ 01202 687237

RINGWOOD
4U Productions
240 Hurn Road, Matchams
☎ 01425 480855 /
461244

SALISBURY
The Chapel Night Club
36 Milford Street
☎ 01722 504255

SWANAGE
Victoria Club
1 High Street
☎ 01929 424944

WEYMOUTH
Harry's
3-5 Maiden Street
☎ 01305 783829

TOURIST INFORMATION CENTRES

Southern Tourist Board
40 Chamberlayne Road, Eastleigh, Hampshire
☎ 02380 620006

ALDERSHOT
Military Museum, Queens Avenue
☎ 01252 320968

ALTON
7 Cross and Pillory Lane
☎ 01420 88448

AMESBURY
Redworth House, Flower Lane
☎ 01980 622833

ANDOVER
Town Mill House, Bridge Street
☎ 01264 324320

AVEBURY
The Great Barn
☎ 01672 539425

BASINGSTOKE
Willis Museum, Old Town Hall, Market Place
☎ 01256 817618

BATH
Abbey Chambers, Abbey Church Yard
☎ 01225 477101

BLANDFORD
Marsh & Ham Car Park, West Street
☎ 01258 454770

BOURNEMOUTH
Westover Road
☎ 09068 020234

BRADFORD-ON-AVON
34 Silver Street
☎ 01225 865797

BRIDPORT
32 South Street
☎ 01308 424901

BRISTOL
St Nicholas Church, St Nicholas Street
☎ 01179 260767

CHIPPENHAM
The Citadel, Bath Road
☎ 01249 706333

CHRISTCHURCH
23 High Street
☎ 01202 471780

DEVIZES
39 St John's Street
☎ 01380 729408

DORCHESTER
Unit 11, Antelope Walk
☎ 01305 267992

EASTLEIGH
Town Hall Centre Leigh Road
☎ 02380 641261

FAREHAM
Westbury Manor, West Street
☎ 01329 221342

FLEET
The Harlington Centre, Fleet Road
☎ 01252 811151

FORDINGBRIDGE
Salisbury Street
☎ 01425 654560

GOSPORT
Gosport Museum, Walpole Road
☎ 02392 522944

HAVANT
1 Park Road South
☎ 02392 480024

HAYLING ISLAND
Beachlands sea front
☎ 02392 467111

LYME REGIS
Guildhall Cottage, Church Street
☎ 01297 442138

LYMINGTON
St Barb Museum & Visitor Centre, New Street
☎ 01590 689000

LYNDHURST & THE NEW FOREST
New Forest Museum, Main Car Park, High Street, Lyndhurst
☎ 02380 282269

MALMESBURY
Town Hall, Market Lane
☎ 01666 823748

MARLBOROUGH
Car Park, George Lane
☎ 01672 513989

MELKSHAM
Church Street
☎ 01225 707424

MERE
The Square
☎ 01747 861211

PETERSFIELD
County Library, 27 The Square
☎ 01730 268829

POOLE
4 Lower High Street
☎ 01202 253253

PORTSMOUTH
The Hard
☎ 02392 826722

102 Commercial Road
☎ 02392 838382

RINGWOOD
The Furlong
☎ 01425 470896

ROMSEY
1 Latimer Street
☎ 01794 512987

ROWNHAMS
M27 Services (Westbound)
☎ 02380 730345

SALISBURY
Fish Row
☎ 01722 334956

SHAFTESBURY
8 Bell Street
☎ 01747 853514

SHERBORNE
3 Tilton Court, Digby Road
☎ 01935 815341

SOUTHAMPTON
9 Civic Centre Road
☎ 02380 221106

SOUTHSEA
Clarence Esplanade
☎ 02392 832464

SWANAGE
The White House, Shore Road
☎ 01929 422885

SWINDON
37 Regent Street
☎ 01793 530328

TROWBRIDGE
St Stephen's Place
☎ 01225 777054

WAREHAM
Trinity Church South Street
☎ 01929 552740

WARMINSTER
Central Car Park
☎ 01985 218548

WELLS
Town Hall, Market Place
☎ 01749 672552

WEYMOUTH
The King's Statue, The Esplanade
☎ 01305 785747

WIMBORNE MINSTER
29 High Street
☎ 01202 886116

WINCHESTER
Guildhall, The Broadway
☎ 01962 840500

MORE INFORMATION

REGIONAL NEWSPAPERS

Local newspapers and periodicals that may be of interest to the visitor include: *Dorset Evening Echo, Dorchester Guardian, Dorset Life,*

The Daily Echo, The Southern Daily Echo, and *Young Wessex*. These are widely available at local newsagents and may be useful in giving up-to-the-minute information.

TELEVISION

The two local television stations for the Southern region include BBC South and Meridian (ITV).

RADIO

There are many local radio stations available, including:

BBC Radio Solent *(96.1 FM and 999 MW)*; Capital Gold *(1170 and 1557 AM)*; Classic Gold *(828 AM)*; Ocean FM *(96.7 and 97.5 FM)*; Power FM *(103.2 FM)*; Spire FM *(102 FM)*; 2CR-FM *(102.3 FM)* and Wessex FM *(96 and 97.2 FM)*.

OTHER USEFUL ADDRESSES

English Heritage
429 Oxford Street,
London
☎ 0207 973 3434

Hampshire & Isle of Wight Wildlife Trust
8 Romsey Road,
Eastleigh, Hampshire
☎ 02380 613636

The National Trust (Southern Region)
Polesden Lacey,
Dorking, Surrey
☎ 01372 453401

West Sussex Environment Agency
Guildbourne House,
Worthing, West Sussex
☎ 01903 820692

ACCOMMODATION

Because of the rich diversity of accommodation available in Britain, ranging from simple camping and caravan sites and holiday camps to bed and breakfast establishments, guest houses and a wide range of hotels of all classes, visitors will generally find it easy to book their accommodation beforehand. Tourist Information Centres (opposite) offer extensive lists of locally available accommodation and many operate a book-a-bed-ahead scheme for travellers.

HOW TO GET THERE

ROAD LINKS

Road access to the South is excellent. The M25, M3, M23 and M27 motorways link the area to all of the major motorway networks of the North, the Midlands, London and the East and West.

Once off the motorways, there is a good network of 'A' roads serving the region, making all the main centres easily accessible.

Some of the more remote areas are only accessible along country lanes (which can be narrow at times and require special care), but generally, the network of roads within the region is excellent.

PARKING IN THE SOUTH

The general rule when parking in this, as in any other region of Britain, is to leave your car at a designated car park and walk to your destination. Do not expect always to be able to park exactly where you want. Take care when parking in narrow roads to avoid causing inconvenience to other road users.

Most people who come to the South do so because they want to escape the pressures of urban life and are more than happy to walk a few extra yards. With this in mind, some of the locations described in this guide are a little way from a convenient car park. Always allow a little extra time to include a walk to and from your car where

necessary. For details of parking permits and location of car parks contact the relevant Tourist Information Centres (opposite).

RAIL LINKS

There is a good rail network serving all parts of the South, linking the area with London and all other major regions. This is supported by a good local network of services. Until recently, all of Britain's rail network came under the auspices of the nationalized British Rail, but this has now been broken up into several individual private companies. It is not always necessary to break long journeys when crossing between regions, but each company has a slightly different operating procedure. If in doubt, check at local stations. There is a direct rail link from London,

Waterloo. A fast network of Inter-City trains also connects several towns in the region to all other regions of Britain.

National Rail Enquiries
☎ 08457 484950

Rail Ticket Sales
☎ 08457 125625

International Rail Enquiries
☎ 08705 848848

South West Trains Ltd
☎ 02380 728162 / 213600

Channel Tunnel Rail Enquiries
Eurostar passenger services
☎ 08705 186186

Vehicle enquiries
☎ 08705 353535

AIRPORTS

In addition to being reasonably close to both Heathrow and Gatwick airports, the South is also served by three regional international airports. For more details of flights available, contact the numbers listed below.

Bournemouth International Airport
☎ 01202 364000

Bristol International Airport
☎ 01275 474444

Southampton International Airport
☎ 02380 620021

PUBLIC TRANSPORT

Public transport in the South is good locally, but most services operate within a limited catchment area and several operate during the summer months only. For local timetable information contact the relevant Tourist Information Centre in the first instance. They will be able to give you the contact number for local bus operatives. For general enquiries regarding local public transport, telephone the following enquiry help lines:

Dorset Passenger Transport
☎ 01305 225165

Southern National
(For local bus services)
☎ 01305 783645

Wiltshire & Dorset Bus Company Hotline
☎ 01202 673555 (Dorset)
☎ 01722 336855 (Wiltshire)

Yellow Buses Information Hotline
☎ 01202 636060

COACH OPERATORS

Britain has several extensive networks of private coach companies which run regular services to the main towns of the South and to all other regions. The following companies operate within the area:

National Express Coach Services
☎ 08705 808080

Stagecoach
☎ 08702 433711

EXCURSIONS

Several coach companies also run excursions to places of interest throughout the region. Check with your hotel or local tour operator, or contact the nearest Tourist Information Centre for details (see page 42).

FERRIES

Several ferry services operate out of South coast ports. Crossings to mainland Europe are offered by the following companies:

Brittany Ferries
(From Portsmouth to St Malo, Caen; Poole to Cherbourg; Plymouth to Roscoff and Santander)
☎ 08705 360360

P&O European Ferries
(From Portsmouth to Le Havre, Cherbourg and Bilbao)
☎ 08705 980555

Swansea to Cork Ferries
☎ 0800 783 8004

For crossings to the Channel Islands and the Isle of Wight:

Condor Ferries
(From Poole to Guernsey and Jersey; Weymouth to Guernsey and St Malo)
☎ 01305 761551

Hovertravel
(passenger)
Portsmouth to Isle of Wight (Ryde)
☎ 01983 811000

Whitelink
Lymington to Yarmouth (Isle of Wight)
☎ 08705 827744

CAR RENTAL

All of the major car rental companies operate in the South, but there are also many local companies offering competitive rates. Our advice is to shop around.

DISABLED TRAVELLERS

For help with all aspects of local, national and international transport for the disabled, contact this number:
☎ 08457 585641

FOR OVERSEAS VISITORS

DRIVING

Always ensure that you have the necessary driving permits and insurance before driving in Britain. Drive on the left side of the road; at roundabouts, give way to the right, unless otherwise instructed. Signposting is generally very good, but you should purchase a copy of the Highway Code for clarification. Road surfaces are generally excellent. Use designated car parks whenever possible and never park on double yellow lines on the road edge.

HEALTH CARE

Before travelling to Britain you should ensure that you have been suitably inoculated (according to your country of origin). There are no prevalent infectious diseases in Britain and no vaccinations are required. The water is safe to drink straight from the tap. While here, you will be entitled to free health care at National Health Service hospitals, although some, or all, of the cost may be recharged to you if your country of origin does not have a reciprocal arrangement with Britain. Please note that dental and eye care is not free.

VAT REFUNDS

Overseas visitors can apply for a refund of VAT for purchases over £50. Ask for a form when making your purchase.

ELECTRICITY

The electricity supply in Britain uses 240 volts AC. Plug adaptors are available in most electrical appliance stores.

TIPPING

There is no formal system of tipping in Britain, and it remains a debatable issue. Generally, a tip of about 10% is acceptable at restaurants, hairdressers and for taxi drivers. Hotel porters might expect a £1 coin tip. Elsewhere tipping is not generally expected, although this is, of course, up to the individual. Some restaurants include a tip (called a service charge) in the bill.

WEATHERLINE

Because of the influence of the winds coming off the Channel, the weather in the South can be very changeable. It is always a good idea to take the appropriate clothing to cover any eventuality if you intend being out for most of the day, especially when walking or cycling. It is also advisable to check the latest local weather forecast for an update before leaving, to make your trip as safe and enjoyable as possible. For up-to-the-minute weather forecasts, call the South Weather Line.
☎ 0891 505303

WALKING & CYCLING

ORDNANCE SURVEY MAPS

You are strongly advised to equip yourself with good maps if you intend venturing out into the countryside, which can be surprisingly remote. Ordnance Survey publish an excellent series of *Outdoor Leisure* maps (Sheets 15 and 22: Purbeck & South Dorset and The New Forest, respectively) at a scale of 1:25,000 (2.5 inches to 1 mile/4cm to 1 km). These maps are ideal for walking because they show such details as contours, Public Rights of Way and tourist information. For a good overview of the area, Sheets 8 and 9 in the Ordnance Survey *Travelmaster* series are ideal.

GETTING OUT & ABOUT

One of the finest ways to explore any region is to use the Public Rights of Way that criss-cross every part of the country. Britain possesses a unique network of some 120,000 miles (193,080 km) of public footpaths, bridleways and byways, most crossing private land. This fascinating network of paths was not created in recent ages for recreational purposes, but is rooted firmly in history, some perhaps being as much as 4,000 years old. They formed part of the highways network in the past, used by villagers to get to work or church, or by traders carrying their wares. They are still maintained as highways by local authorities and are protected in law. Often located in beautiful, remote countryside, these paths are the best way to see Britain.

TYPES OF PATH

There are three main types of Public Right of Way:

Footpaths
For use on foot only.
Bridleways
For use on foot, horseback or bicycle.
Byways
For use on foot, horseback, bicycle or in any other vehicle. Most are unmade surfaces and are waymarked by yellow, blue and red arrows respectively.

Please note:
Cyclists should never use footpaths. They are only legally entitled to use bridleways, byways or other carriageways.

KNOW YOUR RIGHTS

Although the Local Highways Authority is responsible for maintaining Public Rights of Way, it rarely owns the land over which the paths run. Landowners, therefore, can claim a greater right of use and are permitted to plough cross-field paths, provided they are reinstated within two weeks (although headland paths should never be ploughed). It is illegal to obstruct a path or otherwise prevent someone from using it, and all irregularities should be reported to the Local Highways Authority. Paths can be legally diverted or stopped up, however, although notices must be posted and new routes waymarked. A map showing all Public Rights of Way is maintained by the relevant Highways Authority and can usually be consulted at any reasonable time. The routes shown in this guide were accurate at the time of going to press, but things can change. If you are in any doubt about your rights, or the routes, please contact the relevant Highways Authority on the telephone number given below:

Hampshire County Council
☎ 01962 841841

New Forest District Council
☎ 02380 285000

Dorset County Council
☎ 01305 251000

When using the Public Rights of Way network, please always show care and consideration for landowners and people living in the locality (especially when parking) and follow the Country Code (see page 46) at all times.

WHAT TO TAKE

The pull-out walks and cycle rides selected in this guide have been specially devised so that they are suitable even for the inexperienced. It is usually best to travel as light as possible, but always wear appropriate footwear and clothing. Although those places selected here have at least some facilities, it is usually best to assume that none will be available. Plan your itinerary accordingly and take essential supplies and refreshments with you in case, for any reason, they are not available on the route. Remember to tell someone where you are planning to go, in case of an accident. Although some may prefer the solace of lone walking or cycling, it is usually better to take at least one companion (or a mobile phone) in case of emergency. Additionally, you should always take the relevant Ordnance Survey map.

ADDITIONAL INFORMATION FOR SAFE CYCLING

Always ensure your bicycle is in good working order. Take great care on the roads, especially with right turns; if necessary, dismount and cross the road on foot. When out riding, it is essential to wear bright clothing, carry lights and take waterproofs. Always carry refreshments, a small tool kit, puncture repair kit, first-aid kit and enough money for emergencies. Stay alert at all times: be ready for pedestrians on narrow lanes and fast traffic on main roads. Finally, always follow the advice given in the Highway Code.

THE COUNTRY CODE

- **Enjoy the countryside and respect its life and work.**
- **Guard against all risk of fire.**
- **Leave all gates as you find them.**
- **Keep all dogs under close control.**
- **Keep to public paths across farmland.**
- **Use gates and stiles to cross fences, hedges and walls.**
- **Leave livestock, crops and machinery alone.**
- **Take your litter home.**
- **Help to keep all water clean.**
- **Protect wildlife, plants and trees.**
- **Take special care on country roads.**
- **Make no unnecessary noise.**

WHEN THINGS GO WRONG

IF YOU ARE UNWELL

For routine accidents or health problems, contact the local hospital of the region you are staying in. Local doctors will also usually see visitors—contact your nearest Tourist Information Centre for details or ask at your hotel or a chemist shop if necessary. General information on NHS services and treatments is available from:

National Health Service
☎ 0800 665544

EMERGENCIES

In the case of genuine emergencies only, dial 999, free of charge. Speak slowly and clearly and give the operator details of which service you require: Ambulance, Police, Fire Brigade or Coastguard.

POLICE

For all non-urgent police matters, contact the local police station in the area where you are staying.

LIFEGUARDS

Several local authorities now provide lifeguard services at beaches within their control. If you see someone in difficulty in the water, always contact the lifeguard where possible rather than attempt a rescue yourself.

MONEY MATTERS

BANKS

The list of banks and building societies throughout the South would be too lengthy to include here. Most of the larger towns throughout the region will have branches of these institutions, including the four main banks (Barclays, HSBC, National Westminster and Lloyds). Tourist Information Centres can give you a complete list of branches of all banks or building societies.

BUREAU DE CHANGE

Most banks and building societies operate a foreign money exchange service. Check with individual branches for details. Note that travellers' cheques and Eurocheques are widely accepted at shops and restaurants.

CREDIT CARDS

All major credit and debit cards are accepted throughout Britain, including Visa, Mastercard, American Express, Diners, Switch and Delta.

ACKNOWLEDGEMENTS

We would like to thank: Barbara Croucher, Jackie Gaff, David Hobbs,
Ross Kempson and Elizabeth Wiggans for their assistance.
Copyright © 2000 ticktock Publishing Ltd.
First published in Great Britain by ticktock Publishing Ltd., The Offices in the Square, Hadlow, Tonbridge, Kent
TN11 0DD, Great Britain. All rights reserved.
No part of this publication may be reproduced, stored in a retrieval system, or transmitted in any form or by any
means, electronic, mechanical, photocopying, recording or otherwise, without prior written permission of the
copyright owner.
A CIP catalogue record for this book is available from the British Library. ISBN 1 86007 136 8

Picture research by Image Select. Printed in Hong Kong.

Picture Credits: t=top, b=bottom, c=centre, l=left, r=right

David Bailey; 5cr, 19cr, 20cl, 21cl, 35tr & 41t. David Sellman; 3cl, 26cl, 27br, 32/33c. Image Select; OFCtl
& 15b, 2c & 4cl. Greg Evans; OFC (main pic), 3br, 5br, 14bl, 16cr, 19tl, 27tr, 32tl, 33br, 35br, 43c. J. Allan Cash;
OFCc, OFCb, OFCc, IFC & 22c, 6cl, 6bl, 7tr, 15cr, 18cr, 21tr, 34tl. National Trust; 26br. New Forest District
Council; OFCt & 23t, OFCc, 3cr & 36tl, 6tl, 7b, 21b, 22tl, 45t. Pictures Colour Library; 2/3ct, 4br, 18tl.
Spectrum Colour Library; 2cl, 5tl, 7c, 22bl, 22/23cb, 30cr, 34bl, 35cr. West Country Tourist Board; 20br.
The remainder of the images were supplied digitally by Corel Ltd.

The pull-out walks and cycle routes were kindly verified by the Forestry Commission and the Highways Department
of Hampshire, Dorset and Wiltshire County Councils.

ticktock
publishing ltd